LeDoux Vie

The Sweet Life of
John C. LeDoux

Order this book online at www.trafford.com
or email orders@trafford.com

Most Trafford titles are also available at major online book retailers.

Printed in the United States of America.

ISBN: 978-1-4120-0079-6 (sc)

Trafford rev. 07/02/2014

 www.trafford.com
North America & international
toll-free: 1 888 232 4444 (USA & Canada)
fax: 812 355 4082

LEDOUX VIE - The Sweet Life

of

John C. LeDoux

INTRODUCTION

When I was growing up, my Dad and his old WWI buddy, Jack O'Keefe, would get together occasionally. It was really hilarious to listen to these guys recall their old army days and all the crazy things they did. From other sources I knew that Dad had done many things like being a cowboy, a lumberjack, a streetcar conductor, a soldier, and a policeman. I knew only a little about Mom and her life before she was married. I always wished I knew more.

On occasion I would tell the kids my own sea stories. Some of the kids suggested that I should put them down on paper for posterity. So this book is an overview of my life as best I can recall it. It should give you a better understanding of what I have done and where I have been. You may enjoy the funny and unusual things that have happened. You all appreciate my distorted sense of humor.

You will find, I hope, some of the principles that have guided my life. Trust, honesty and a sense of duty to your responsibilities. Be content that you did your best in every situation. The intrinsic rewards should be reward enough. The extrinsic rewards will usually follow. Help those in need if you possibly can. Finally stand up for what you know is right regardless of what the consequences may be. I have found that a person that can do the common things uncommonly well will always be in demand. My favorite guiding scripture is Proverbs 3:6.

"Acknowledge Him in all your ways and He will direct your path".

DEDICATION

This book, as my biography has turned out to be, is lovingly dedicated to the one person primarily responsible for "The Sweet Life" my wife, the mother of all you kids, who thought she would never have any. Her love, understanding, forgiveness and patience are more than I truly deserve.

Sirach 26:1-4 from the Catholic Bible says it all:

Happy the husband of a good wife,
twice lengthened are his days:
A worthy wife brings joy to her husband,
peaceful and full is his life.
A good wife is a generous gift bestowed
upon him who fears the Lord:
So be he rich or poor, his heart is content,
and a smile is ever on his face.

CHAPTER I - THE EARLY YEARS (1924-1926)

First there was a bright light. Then a stinging sensation to my petite derriere and with that I announced my arrival to the LeDoux clan. The place: Portland, Oregon - the date and time, about 10 a.m. on Sunday morning May 18, 1924, happily on my paternal grandmother's birthday. The records do not say what the weather was like but that was of little concern to me since I did not even know what weather was. All I knew was that I had left a very secure and comfortable environment into a strange and noisy one.

Some time later I was to learn that I was the second offspring born to Edith Lillian (Carver) LeDoux, aged 24, and John Francis LeDoux, aged 26. My older sister Edith, who went by Dede, had arrived two years previously and now occupied the supreme position of eldest sibling. She must have not been jealous of me for she took good care of me as evidenced by several photos where she was **holding my hand** and guiding me safely for some unknown destination. However, one photo of Dede's unhappy expression as she stands besides Mom holding my hand might indicate otherwise. In later years we had some moments of disagreements like the time she almost hit me with a dining room chair. Dad unexpectedly came home for lunch and rescued me. We loved each other very much and still do.

As time progressed I learned that I was part of a very prolific clan. Dad was a twin (Anna Frances) and had 12 other brothers and sisters. Mom had 10 brothers and sisters. She was an English WWI war bride as Dad was a soldier and served overseas during World War I. So you can see Dede and I had 22 aunts and uncles. Three of the girls become nuns and Arthur died at age 4yr-10months. In spite of this, between our English and American aunts and uncles who married we had over 120 first cousins.

John Francis was the 10th of the brood. From what I can find out he was quite energetic and got into a lot of trouble. He joined the National Guard when he was 17 or 18 and went overseas with the Rainbow Division in 1917. As far as I can tell he did not see any combat since he seemed to be in trouble as a soldier, was on KP most of the time as discipline. His record shows a number of summary courts martial. He did receive an honorable discharge at war's end. He worked as a cowboy, logger, and street car conductor before we moved to California in 1926. He was a police officer for many years with an outstanding record of catching a number of criminals. He was one of only twelve officers selected for the Alameda County Kidnap squad (after the Lindberg kidnapping episode). The squad was led by District Attorney Earl Warren whose influence later on had an impact on my career. We have a packet of information about his police career if anyone wishes to see it.

As mentioned above Mom (Edith Lillian LeDoux) was from Liverpool, England. She was very petite, only 4 ft 8 in - quite beautiful and a talented singer. When I was quite young she sang on the radio for a local station. It is noteworthy that my Dad had met Mom's sister Elsie first. Once he met Edith all thoughts of Elsie evaporated. Elsie joked about that but she accepted it without rancor. So after the war, Mom come over from England about 1920 the year they were married. Even though she lived in California most of her life, she never lost all of her British accent. She also had a typical British sense of humor. Minutes after a funny story was told and we had gone on to something else, she would

burst out laughing when she finally figured out the punch line. She also used to laugh and say "I don't get it". She was a doll and was loved by all who knew her. I still get sentimental whenever I hear the song "Danny Boy" one of her favorites. **Married Nov 3 1920.**

Sorry for the digression but you all need to know a little about your forebears. They were both great parents.

What do I remember about Portland? Not much. Remember I was only two years old when we went south to California. I do remember a few things. We lived near Grandma's house. My Grandfather was in the construction business and worked his way from Wisconsin to Oregon

building railroads. I understand he worked on many of the major buildings in Portland. He built the house that Grandma occupied. He died in 1920 so I never knew him. I vaguely remember Grandma because I was always going over to Grandma's house. I do remember sitting in her ample lap.

Near our house, maybe a block away was a house or apartment that had a stucco type exterior but with many colored stones in it. This really fascinated two children. I loved to pick off the colored stones. Also near us was Peninsula Park. with trees, ponds, swimming pool, bandstand and lots of boxwood bushes and roses. Whenever I smell boxwood I think of that park. Twice Dede saved me from drowning in the pond and in the swimming pool. Drowning as I remember it is not unpleasant. You just sort of go to sleep. **Jack and Dede on left.**

The final episode was almost fatal. Apparently I was eating some lamb chops and a small piece of bone became stuck in my lung. It wouldn't come loose and I began to waste away. I guess they could not operate for that in those days. Grandma prayed for me and some months later on the Feast of Corpus Christi, I coughed it up and handed it to my mother.

Hazards to the young were many in those days. Before I was two I came close to dying three times. The Lord had other plans for all my progeny.

Speaking of progeny, take a look at the F.X. LeDoux family, my grandfather and his 12 living children. Arthur died at 4. My Dad is #2 on 2nd row in his army uniform. Dated August 1917.

This is my Mom's family, the Carvers in England in 1949. She's at center.

CHAPTER II - THE GOLDEN STATE (1926 - 1943)

We moved to California in 1926 or 1927. I suppose my Dad moved at the urging of his brother Frank who was then living in California. I have no memory of the move but we must have traveled by car.

San Leandro at this time was a small town just South of Oakland. The population was about 10,000. It was renowned for its flowers and fruit. The mild year round climate was an added plus. Our first house was on St. Mary's Avenue. We lived in a single floor little stucco house. The Frank and Margaret LeDoux family also lived on this same street.

We lived on St.Mary's before I went to school so I only have a few vague memories of that period. At one point I had two large dogs. I do remember how bad I felt when they both died either from poison or dog fights. Another incident I do remember. At the end of the street was a utility ditch about 2 feet deep. All the kids were playing around it when someone threw a rock that hit me in the back of the head. Apparently the injury bled profusely as my shirt was covered with blood. I know that Mom was quite concerned but it really was not that bad.

We moved a number of times before the folks bought a house at 285 West Broadmoor. We had lived a block over on Garcia in an apartment for a time. Two other houses come to mind; one with a number of fruit trees in the back yard, on the corner of Haas and Woodland. We also had a little dog that was poisoned by a neighbor just the day before we were going on vacation. I am not sure why we moved but all the places seemed OK to me. The 285 house was bought in the middle 30s for a grand sum of about $4500 with a mortgage of $32 per month.

POLICEMAN DAD

During most of this time Dad was a police officer. According to news articles he was a very good one with the intuition of a Jessica Fletcher. He apprehended some rough characters who had stolen Herbert Marshall's (the movie star) car in Beverly Hills two weeks previously. Dad spotted the car heading toward Oakland and something just didn't look right. Once he arrested Tom Mix (cowboy star) for speeding. We got free tickets to his wild West show and met him after the show.

THE BROADMOOR GANG

We had about 10 or 12 kids in our gang at West Broadmoor. The Bradow family lived across the street. Alan was about 4 years older than me. He was like an older brother to me and we have been friends all our lives. I last saw Alan in 1988. We really had a good time recalling all the crazy things we did.

When we first moved to 285, there were two empty lots to our left. The Bradow's house across the street had a large empty lot to their right, about 10 to 12 lots. Behind their house was a farm of about

60 acres. Dad borrowed a bulldozer and cleared that field for a baseball diamond. We always played baseball, football, cowboys and Indians until way past dark. Our baseball games went 15 or 16 innings, night after night. Usually the game broke up when the Dunsfords (next door neighbors) had to go home and took the bat and ball with them. That was real sandlot ball. We never had any parents present at any of these sporting events. Thank God!

We roamed far and wide. About a mile to the West was a railroad line and bridge trestle. We always took a handful of double headed nails with us to the railroad to make small swords. If you put the nails on the tracks, the train would flatten them and they looked just like a sword. Sometimes we would see hobos below the trestle but we avoided them.

HILL HIKING

To the East about 3 miles were the San Leandro hills - about as high as some of the mountains here in Virginia. During the summer months we would often get up early, pack a lunch, and off to the hills we would go. There was a really neat stream up there, probably part of San Leandro Creek. It was about 15 to 20 feet wide with large rocks in the center. The water moved pretty quick but we

managed to get on the rocks to eat our lunch. The water was cold and drinkable. We did drink from it with no problem

.We were all **bow and arrow shooters** and sometimes we would take our bows into the hills. I had a 40 lb bow that would shoot about 200 yards. We would position ourselves across a gully and shoot arrows at each other - high shots that we could see and avoid most of the time. A few times arrows would be lost in the haze and land a few feet away.. Stupid, but kids will be kids. **Note Gary with fingers in ears.**

We used to make wooden swords and shields and play King Arthur. Our battles would cover many blocks. We had some really good fights. Remember all this was long before TV so we had to do something. Sunday nights were the big radio nights when we all sat around to listen to Fibber McGee and Molly, Jack Benny, and Fred Allen. Then there were the spooky shows like "The Shadow" and the "Creaking Door". Really quite scary.

These shows must have affected us. One day Alan, Shirley, Dede and I were doing the dishes when we heard what we thought were footsteps coming down the stairs. Nobody else was in the house. So we got brave and armed with bats or knives we went as a group to find out who was there. The stairs were around the corner from the kitchen and when we came around that corner, nobody was there. We slowly crept up the stairs to the bedroom on the right because in its closet was a half door to the attic. We opened the closet door and sat on the bed since we were convinced that the person or ghost must surely be in the attic.

We nervously waited on the bed for 5 or 10 minutes and nothing happened. Then the door to the attic began to slowly open. With one accord we screamed and beat a hasty retreat down the stairs and out of the house. Like UFOs today, there never was an explanation of the footsteps or the opening of that attic door. You think TV is scary? Try footsteps and attic doors!

Back in those days there were no super markets. We had two small family owned grocery stores two blocks East on East 14th street. One was Sam's and the other was the Belleview Market. Sam was really good to the kids. He had a penny candy counter that you would have to see to believe. In those days a nickel or a dime could buy you a bag full of candy. Of course we made our choices very carefully and must have driven Sam nuts over our protracted buying methods.

PICKING CHERRIES

As I mentioned, San Leandro was noted for flowers and fruits. I think it was even called the Cherry City. One of our favorite summer activities was getting on our bikes and go cherry picking. This had to be done at night and usually clandestinely. We would find an orchard (not hard to do), park our bikes in the dark and climb trees to pick a big bag of cherries. Then we would go home and sit on the curb to feast on our loot. One time we were nearly caught by the orchard owners. There were about five of us and the owners heard us, I guess. They came out loudly proclaiming that they would find these cherry picking thieves. I was laying on the ground and was almost stepped on by one of the men. They went inside and we high tailed out of there as fast as we could. I think they saw us but were just trying to scare us. It worked!

Back in those days, no one had refrigerators. We had ice boxes. The ice in 25 lbs pieces would be put in the upper chamber and food in the lower chamber. The melted ice would drain in a container near the floor. The ice man would cut a piece for each house and deliver it to the ice box. This would take about 5 minutes. During this time we would raid the truck for the pieces of ice on the floor. Better than a popsicle any day.

THE PUTT-PUTT BOAT GAMBIT (About 1935)

One of our biggest adventures was the putt-putt boat gambit. A putt-putt boat was a small metal boat about 8 inches long. It was like a small cabin cruiser. In the roof was a small boiler which you filled with water. In the cabin area you put a little flat candle. The candle would heat the water, and the resulting steam would escape through two little pipes that exited from the stern of the boat propelling it along at good speed.

What a marvelous toy for small boys! We all had to have one. An ad in the paper told us that the Woolworth store in Oakland had them for 15 cents. What a deal! Somehow about 8 of us managed to scrape up the 15 cents but the Oakland store was over 10 miles away. Alan, our leader, told us that the local 5&Dime store in San Leandro must have putt-putt boats. That store was only 1 mile to the South while Oakland was to the North.

The next day our hardy band of 8 (ranging from about six to 15 years old) took off about 8 a.m. for the local 5&Dime. We did not bother to tell our parents where we were going. After all we would be back in less than an hour. We arrived at the store about 8:30 and there they were. Beautiful little red and blue boats! Then disaster struck! The price at this store was 20 cents. Getting another nickel was out of the question.

Our illustrious leader then declared that we would just have to go to Oakland now 11 miles away. It was a beautiful day - what was a measly 11 miles to a bunch of kids. There was a streetcar on East 14th Street that went all the way to downtown Oakland but that would take two 10 cent fares. We had no choice but to hoof it.

We reached Lake Merritt about 2 p.m. The store was still about a mile away. The little kids were about out of steam so we told them they could wait by the lake and the older 2 or 3 would go get the boats. We got to the store and bought 8 boats for 15 cents each.. We returned to the lake and picked up the little ones and started back to San Leandro. We did not hit the panic button until we were about halfway there and it was about 5 p.m. Remember we had no lunch and our parents had no idea where we were.

We held a council of war. Alan and I decided that we would hurry back home and send someone back for the rest of the group. We ran a block and walked a block, rested some and continued until we got home about 8 p.m. We never could understand why our parents were so upset. After all we were OK. Look at our putt-putt boats! I guess they sent cars after the rest of the troop and all's well that ends well. Imagine kids trying to do that today. We had to go through some pretty tough neighborhoods but were never bothered by anyone. Recently I saw as ad for Putt-Putt boats just like the ones we had but now the price was $19.95. So I bought one anyway.

THE FISHPOND CAPER

Those boats lasted a long time. We played with them in Billy and Jimmy Dunsford's fish pond. Their house was next to ours. This pond played another role later on that was really hilarious and I still have to laugh when I think about it.

I can't remember the kid's name, but he was really obnoxious. He was visiting one of the guys. Sometimes at night we would play kick the can. The whole neighborhood was available. During one of the escape sequences of the game about 4 of us ran from the street to our back yard. We vaulted our fence into the Dunsford yard, skirted the pond and ran on. We didn't think to warn this visitor about the pond. He vaulted the fence and went directly into the pond. Have you ever seen a wet puppy? That's what he looked like. We all laughed so hard we almost got sick. The game ended right there.

HALLOWEEN HIJINKS

One of our favorite times was Halloween. We never did believe in the treat part but the tricks were really fun. I won't tell all the things we did so the grandkids won't get some wrong ideas but some of the tricks weren't fun for the trickees.

The simplest trick was ringing doorbells without waiting for the response. We got some strong black fishing line and attached it to the screen door (most houses had simple screen doors without locks). One of us would silently sneak up to the door, attach the line to the handle, ring the bell and then hide near the porch. The occupants would come to the door and find no one there. With a puzzled look, they closed the front door. At that precise moment we would use the line to make the screen door open and close a few times. The front door would open and again the occupant would find no one there. This really puzzled them. We would do this once or twice and then break the line and go on to the next victim. This was supposed to make people think there were real ghosts on Halloween.

Of course there were always a few yard gates that could be removed and hung on nearby telephone poles. We would also write messages on car windows with wax. This was quite difficult to remove.

Remember the 60 acre field? One of the crops grown there were tomatoes. By Halloween most of the tomatoes had been picked but there was always lots of rather ripe ones left in the field. We would gather a supply and sit on the curb waiting for an opportunity to use some. Invariably some teenagers would come by in a car and yell at us and throw something at us, usually tomatoes. Little did they realize that our baseball throwing arms were very accurate and we would pepper the car with ripe tomatoes and then escape in the darkness of the adjacent field. By the way, the car throwers never came close to hitting us with their ammunition.

One of the not so nice episodes with the tomatoes on Halloween was directed at poor Mr. Norton. He lived a few doors from us and was the block crank. He frequently objected to the loud and boisterous play of the Broadmoor gang. So one Halloween we decided to administer frontier justice. Armed with tomatoes we rang his doorbell one Halloween night. This time we did not use the line trick. When he answered the door, he was standing behind the screen door. Several well aimed tomatoes hit the screen and must have sprayed him with tomato juice. There never was any retribu-

tion because he could never identify the assailants. For several years, a tomato plant would spring up next to his porch.

During the year we used to practice our Halloween bell wringing tactics just to keep in shape. Once a man in pajamas chased us for several blocks yelling obscenities at us. He was no match for the fleet footed Broadmoor gang. As I grew and matured I realized some of these pranks were not very funny to the home owners and I admonish the grand kids not to try any of them.

9

Another popular activity with the gang was to go into the hills and rent horses for riding like **old time cowboys** On one of these rides, I was galloping along when the horse stepped in a hole and went down throwing me over his head. His rear end rolled over on me. The horse got up and galloped away. I got up without any injury. Just a week before, a girl had a similar accident and was killed. This picture shows me as a tough looking cow poke.

THE WICKER CHAIR

One of the gang, Bud Evans, lived at the end of the block. In an attic above the garage, there was an old wicker rocking chair. If you ever look at a piece of wicker, you will see that it is about one-fourth inch in diameter and has a series of small holes running the length of the wicker. We cut a few small pieces off the chair and tried using the wicker like a cigarette. It would burn slowly and the holes provided a pathway for the smoke to come out the end. That was our first try at smoking. We must have done a lot of that because the chair really started to disappear. I figure though that smoking wicker saved me from cigarettes later on. Wicker is some strong smoking stuff and we decided that it was not that much fun.

Eventually, houses were built in the empty lots next to 285. While under construction, we kids would play in them after the workers went home. We would even jump from the second story to the ground. One time we were under the house smoking our wicker when the construction boss came around and saw the smoke. He told us to come out from under there. We replied "Come in and get us." We could only see the lower half of him but we could see him clench his fists and then he stalked away. We left shortly thereafter and never used that location again. As you may know, I never did acquire the smoking habit Praise be to wicker!

For you hot rod enthusiasts take a look at the **family auto about 1930** or so.

This is a shot of my 'brother' Alan.

CHAPTER III - GRAMMAR SCHOOL YEARS (1930-1938)

St. Mary's parochial school. I can still remember that first day. I definitely was not enthusiastic about it. The school building seemed immense, two or three stories high. We entered through a gate into the girls' play yard. The boys and girls were separated for play. The building was L-shaped with two doors on the wing to the right. I remember swing sets on the left. I guess Mom took me into the first grade room (no pre-school in those days) and introduced me to Sister Claire. The nuns were Dominicans with habits of black and white. The **head gear was like a big arc over their heads**, ending almost to their shoulders. They were truly awesome figures to a six year old. I do remember Dede rescuing me that first day after Mom left. I did not want to be separated from Dede by going to the boys' play yard so she took me into the girls' yard that first day. Do not know if she was punished for it but I must have adapted.

I found out later that this was Sister Claire's first class. She was truly quite beautiful and I fell in love with her. In 1988, I visited her in San Rafael when they had a special Mass for her. Imagine seeing your first grade teacher after 58 years. She still looked great.

St. Mary's was across town from 285. I suppose Mom drove me initially but I eventually walked and then rode my bike when I got one about age 12. It seemed like it was at least 2 miles maybe further but we all walked or rode bikes. Dede claims it was only a mile. About one block from school was a path leading to a long wooden bridge that spanned San Leandro Creek. Then through a residential neighborhood and eventually to East 14th Street (the main street through town). It took 30 to 40 minutes to walk and 15 to 20 minutes on the bike.

Once while Dede and I were riding our bikes to school, we were pedaling furiously since we were running late. Dede was near the curb and I was on the outside. She had her head down and somehow ran into a parked car. Books, Dede and bike were all over the place. I guess she was not seriously hurt and to my shame I was more concerned about the bike than I was about her. We finally made it to school and Dede's teacher's only remark "Better late than never" summed up the event.

There was no cafeteria. We all brought our lunches. The cloak room had that distinctive lunch bag odor from the 25 or so lunches. At lunch we ate in the play yards, weather permitting. We played games after eating with one that sticks in my mind. The game was to run from one side to the other without being tagged or caught by several boys in the middle. Good practice for learning to dodge.

I was one of those selected for crossing patrol. We had badges and army type caps to wear. It was a honor to be one especially if your Dad was a real cop. The Chief of Police would come and talk to us at the beginning of each year. I was a LT when I was in the eighth grade.

St. Leander's Church was just across the street from the school. I was an altar boy for several years. Had to get up early for the 6 a.m. Mass and ride my bike to the church. During the week we wore the black and white gowns and on Sunday the red and white ones. It was fun although learning all that Latin was not. The peculiar fragrance of the wines and incense and vestments was unique. I think my name is still on a WWII brass plaque. Most every boy in my class and in high school served during WWII. Bud Evans ended up in a wheel chair. Len Messenger died aboard the Indianapolis.

Discipline was tight with the nuns so I don't remember any pranks. When we graduated we were well grounded in reading, writing (grammar and spelling), and math. I must have done OK since I was awarded a scholarship to the Christian Brothers High School in Berkeley.

While in grammar school, I had several paper routes. One was a weekly advertiser that we put on the porches of every house. We had to get there about 5 a.m. to get the papers and deliver before 7. I boxed the papers and threw them on the porch from my moving bike. Could throw left or right with great accuracy. I had to deliver about 200 papers for $1.00. One morning the boss showed up and told us we had to place the papers on the porches not throw them on.

I responded "You mean I have to get off my bike and place the paper on the porch?" He said "Yes". My final reply "For a measly half cent you can have your route. I quit." He was very angry with me because he was stuck with 200 papers to deliver but I stuck to my guns and walked out.

The next route was with the daily Oakland Inquirer. I had a route near home with 60 papers. Made about $20 per month. This was an afternoon paper so we met at a local garage to pick up our papers and box them before we took off. An old man with a push cart type bike would show up 2 or 3 times a week. His wife baked these fruit pies. They were about 4 inches in diameter but they were real tasty. Cost 25 cents so he made about 15 sales with all the paper boys.

One of my customers was at the end of one street about a half mile from the next house. I had to cross the railroad tracks (remember that rail line?) over an unmarked crossing. The tracks were about

5 feet above the surrounding ground so you had to go over a ramp to cross the tracks. I still had about half my papers left to deliver so I usually pedaled hard as I approached the ramp to let the bike coast over the tracks. There was a corn field on both sides of the tracks and road. One autumn day as I went up the ramp and reached the top I heard this loud whistle and to my left was an oncoming train at high speed. I still remember the black engine with two flags fluttering in the wind. The sight and sound paralyzed me but the bike had enough speed to cross the tracks before the train did. Might have cleared by 50 feet or so. Not once before or after that did I ever see another train. Needless to say, I walked across from then on.

CHAPTER IV - MERRY OLDE ENGLAND

In 1932 , WWI vets were paid a bonus to offset the depression. Mom had left home when she was only 20 and had not seen her relatives since then. So the bonus was used to give her a trip back home. Dede and I were to go too but poor old Dad had to stay home and keep the home fires burning.

This was supposed to be only a summer vacation but we spent most of one year in England. We sailed from San Francisco on a Swedish or Norwegian cargo-passenger ship. There were 12 staterooms for the passengers. As I remember it the ship was truly immaculate and the crew was very friendly. We all ate at the Captain's table. Dede and I were the only children on board so the crew really spoiled us. I remember playing on the hatch covers and watching the sailors do their work - painting, chipping, etc. I think this sea voyage made me want to be a sailor and why I wanted to be in the Navy. **Our Passport photo to right.**

I think the trip to England took almost a month and we went via the Panama Canal. There was a man on board who I think was taken with Mom. She was very pretty and I am sure attracted men. Anyway he always seemed to be around. While going through the Canal, we were able to go ashore at Colon. The main street of Colon is American on one side and Panamanian on the other. We were walking on the Panamanian side. It was very hot. This gentleman just collapsed and fell to the ground. The natives immediately just robbed him of everything they could. The American police came over but could do nothing for him. I guess Mom just hustled us back to the ship since I do not know what happened after that. He died apparently of heatstroke.

Aside from that, the voyage was uneventful but very pleasant. I think we arrived in London not Liverpool and were met by an old friend of Mom's, a Mr. Graham, as I recall. It seems like we saw part of London then. I do remember going to the famous Wax Works. The grisly part that showed some of the famous criminals and their gory ends was very impressive.

We stayed with Mom's parents, the Carvers. They were both very sweet people. Grandpa Carver was some sort of clerk. Grandma was always in the kitchen, the only warm room in the house. They lived in a row house in a street that ended in a culdesac. The house at the end was a large one owned by a more affluent family. Behind our house was a very small yard surrounded by brick walls. Beyond this yard was an alleyway.

Even though Mom had 10 brothers and sisters, I only remember Uncle Bob and Aunts Flo, Renee, and Elsie. I'm sure we met all the others but I can't recall them. I do remember one relative lived on a nice residential area with curving streets. I rode a bike on the sidewalk there and managed to ride right into a Bobby. He was very nice and did not give me a ticket.

We stayed there so long, that we were sent to the local schools. I was the only boy who was wearing long pants. They all wore short pants. This caused some heckling by the Brits and I ended up in a series of short fights with some of them over it. Dad told me when I left for England that I better not lose any fights or else. Remember he and his dirty dozen managed to bust up a few English pubs and the family honor must be upheld.

I guess things settled down and I enjoyed school. The room I was in had double desks so two students were seated together. I cannot remember my seat mate but we must have hit it off. I did have a couple of good friends there before the year was out.

The toy stores in England were fabulous. I had a number of well made toys and a real metal play sword. Dede had a neat toy candy store. The fish and chips you could buy on the streets were also delicious. Grandma also made these small tarts that I could eat all day long

Dede and I slept on the 3rd floor. They did not have central heat and it seems like only the kitchen was warm. The house also had gas lights since electricity was not common then. One night Dede and I were almost gassed because we blew out the flame instead of turning it off. I think Aunt Flo checked on us and saved the day.

One of the interesting things about England during the summer was the very late twilights. Must be the latitude at 53 degrees North vs the 35 to 40 degrees here in the States. Twilight lasted until near 11 at night. The kids in our area played a sort of flashlight tag game - boys against the girls. A game would go on for several nights in succession. We all had flashlights with red, green and white lights. The game would go on until all of one side had been captured. There were many places to hide with the back alleys and so forth. A corner store was the only safe place to get some rest. The red lights on the flashlights (torches in England) would provide a warning to a teammate. The green light signaled that it was safe to move. Lots of fun as I remember it.

Eventually, the visit had to end and we sailed from Liverpool on a real passenger ship. It had all kinds of nice things on it and we had a ball. The passage was only about 5 days to New York and then we spent another 5 days on a train back to California. Dad was very happy to see us although he paid more attention to Mom than to me and Dede. That seemed strange to me at the time but now I understand.. He also was not happy with my new British accent. **The picture above was taken just after we returned from England.**

CHAPTER V - THE TEEN YEARS

Dad and I did a lot of fishing during my younger and teen years. We fished in San Francisco Bay, the Sacramento River, the ocean at Santa Cruz and in the Sierras. While fishing in the Bay one day, we saw one of the first China Clippers take off. This was the start of PanAm. He was the fisherman. I was not that good but loved to be with him. He was a really funny guy. He could tell stories with all the accents. Some of them were a little rough and could embarrass the women. His pantomime of various men going to a public restroom was hilarious. When he and his old war buddy Jack O'Keefe got together it was Katie Bar the Door. They apparently had some really wild times while in the Army. I guess that explains his numerous infractions in his Army record. They were part of a real dirty dozen when in England. Apparently their sole objective was to tear English pubs apart. Though he was only 5'8" and about 180 lbs - he was one tough dude.

I was present at one startling event. I saw him dismantle a police officer who was about 6'2" and well over 200 lbs. The poor guy never had a chance. The background went back several years. While on the force Dad helped an ex Canadian WWI flyer get a job on the police force. McDonald and Dad were friends at one time and somehow McDonald did something foul to Dad. It may have been politics since being on the force was not protected and if you backed the wrong mayor you could be fired. Dede thinks it might have been some jealousy over Mom.

Anyway, what I saw went like this. Dad was no longer on the police force. We were driving South on East 14th Street when we passed McDonald who was on the sidewalk. As we drove past, McDonald gave my Dad the finger. Dad slammed on the brakes, vaulted out of the car, and really cleaned McDonald's clock. It was no contest. Dad was arrested for assaulting a police officer and had to appear before a judge. Judge Bruner was an old friend and his sentence was probation and not fighting with a police officer for six months. I think McDonald left the force shortly thereafter.

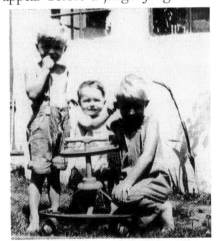

When I was 14 Mom and Dad had **Ronnie.** Shortly thereafter **Gary and Richard** followed. Mom claims they were all just accidents. Though Mom was tiny, she delivered her babies easily - about 20 minutes of hard labor. She became famous at East Oakland Hospital. When she arrived at the door the nurses went into a panic with a cry of "Here's that woman again!"

While I was still home I helped a lot with these kids, changed diapers, put to bed and so forth. Ronnie was the leader of the group and they were always getting into all kinds of Calvin like trouble. I guess I should include a few Ronnie stories for posterity.

When he was about 2, he woke up early one morning, climbed out of bed and decided to go for a walk. He went East on West Broadmoor toward East 14th Street. East 14th is a major artery of 4 lanes plus the two streetcar tracks. Somehow he crossed that busy street and continued South for several blocks. Finally he went up to a house and knocked on the door. The woman who answered the door looked down at this little blond kid and heard "I'm hungry". She fed him and then called the police. Dad was in the station at the time and said "I know who that is. I'll take care of it."

Dad was an exceptional fixer of things. He always had a pair of pliers or a screwdriver in his back pocket. Ronnie, about 4, imitated his Dad and had a small screwdriver in his back pocket. I don't know who was supposed to be watching Ronnie, but one day Mom returned home and found most of the door knobs off the doors. She called for Ronnie and he came running from somewhere and said to her " I fix. I fix." Later that same day, she went to use the oven and the door fell off.

These are all second hand stories, since I had already departed for the Navy. Mom and Dad had a walk in closet upstairs. One day she was doing something in this closet and Ronnie locked her in the closet. Mom asked and finally pleaded with Ronnie to open the door. His reply for over an hour was " In a minute, in a minute."

When he finally let Mom out, she chased him with a coat hanger but he managed to escape by hiding under a bed. Must have stayed there a long time to let Mom cool off.

One story shows his persistence in face of a challenge. Our back yard had the usual 5 ft wooden fence. The one we vaulted the night of the fishing pond episode. When only 3 or so, Ronnie managed to climb over this fence when he was supposed to stay in the yard. Dad added another 4 or 5 ft of height. When finished he turned to Ronnie and said "See what you can do with that you little bugger." As the story goes, Ronnie took only a few minutes to spot a weak spot near a corner. In a flash, he was at the top looking back with a mischievous grin. Somewhere there is a snap shot of the event. I understand that Ronnie carried the same attitude into school and the U.S. Navy endearing himself to persons in authority.

My Dad was fair and firm in discipline. I only remember a few mild spankings. You just knew the rules. One night about 11 p.m. when Gary was about 16 a car horn sounded outside. Dad was reading the paper and Ronnie was watching TV. Gary got up and put on his jacket. Dad says "Where do you think you are going?" Gary says "Out". "It's 11 o'clock, you are not going anywhere!" ordered Dad who steps to the front door. "Out of my way old man" foolishly demands Gary. Dad squares to face Gary and calmly offers a challenge "OK Gary you can have the first hit". Before Ron can warn Gary, he is doing a back somersault as Dad lands a solid body blow. Gary slowly gets up and announces that he is going to bed. Dad sits down and resumes his reading.

When I visited Ronnie in 1988 we went to San Rafael to see my first grade teacher Sister Claire. One of Ronnie's former nuns was also there. Sister Claire greeted me with warmth and enthusiasm. Ronnie's teacher was very reserved and obviously on guard. You could see the alarm in her eyes expecting Ronnie to pull one of his pranks again. It was really funny. Ron and I laughed about the reaction of the two nuns for a long time after that.

On this same trip to California. Ron took me up in the Sierras to see my son Jimmy. He had a rustic cabin in the mountains and we had a time finding him. Ronny wanted to go out that night to a local bar and he never returned. I was worried about him but he showed up in the morning and said his **truck was stuck.** In the dark, he was turning around to go up Jim's mountain road and he nearly backed into a deep ravine. Another Ronny escapade.

This is a picture of me and Ronny when I was about 16. Keeping Ron from going over the fence. **Alan and I with our gliders below.**

CHAPTER VI - HIGH SCHOOL DAZE

My first year in high school was at the Christian Brothers school in Berkeley. The tuition was free due to the scholarship but the bus ride was about an hour and a half both ways. I had to change buses in Oakland. The discipline at the school approached that of boot camp. The teachers were all young brothers and they did not allow any distractions in class. Once, while lecturing, the teacher was walking up and down the aisles. Two of the guys were having a whispered discussion and as the Brother reached one of them, he swept him onto the floor next to his desk. He stepped over the body and never missed a beat in his lecture.

Brother Thomas, our math instructor, once told a boy in the back of the room to move up to the front row so "I won't have to walk so far to hit you." Needless to say we were attentive most of the time. That year gave me a firm educational foundation.

After my freshman year I had to transfer to San Leandro High because of the cost and the long bus rides. Because of the Broadmoor gang and grammar school friends, I knew a number of students at the high school. It was also nice to have girls in the classroom.

At this time I began working at Rush's Meat Market. Alan had worked there and was quitting and he got me hired. Alan was student body president that year. Mr. Rush was the archetype German butcher. When you see the cartoon of the beer barreled, handle bar mustached German you have Mr. Rush. He was the consummate professional. Made all his own sausage, smoked his own ham and bacon, did everything a butcher could do. Customers came from miles around to buy his products. They were fantastic. I have never tasted anything like his sausage and smoked meats. He was very strict and a tough man to work for. I was paid the princely sum of 10 cents per hour and had all the lowly jobs to do. Some years later my Mom took Rush to court since the minimum wage was 25 cents per hour. He had to pay me several hundred dollars and was not very happy.

Besides the usual cleaning and sweeping and trimming meat jobs, I was the main delivery person. Dad made a large basket carrier to put on my bike and twice a day I would take off to deliver meat. It would take me about an hour and a half each time. I didn't mind that as it was a relief to get out from under Mr. Rush.

His son Al, a weight lifter, also worked there. He was OK. Every Saturday night Al, Alan and I would go bowling. Bowling alleys then were low ceilinged, smoky dives unfit for women. It cost 10 cents per game. It did not take long to spend most of my week's wages. We also went squirrel hunting in the hills and valleys.

Even though I was not allowed to do much except grind hamburger, I did learn a lot - the various cuts of meat for beef, pork and lamb. The old man would work in the back doing his sausage thing. All the trimmed meat would go into several large porcelain vats about 3 feet high. The top layers did not look so good, but beneath that was good meat. Old man Rush would combine various combinations of beef, pork and lamb for the various kinds of sausage. These combinations were ground up and inserted into intestine skins and then smoked. He would also prepare pork legs for ham by pumping brine through the leg veins. These were then taken to his smoke house in the valley for slow smoking. I have never since tasted ham as good as his.

BELLEVIEW MARKET

I worked for Rush for about a year and then Ray Williams at the Belleview Meat Market offered me a job. This store was much closer to home and he offered me $1.00 per hour. That was 10x what I was getting at Rush's so naturally I accepted. Ray was 28 at the time and his father Bill was in his 50s with a heart condition. Ray was a real professional and a hard worker. I worked for him about 2 years from 1940 to 1942.

Naturally I did all the hard and dirty work like cleaning the bloody large walk in refrigerator. But he took we under his wing and taught me the business. In those days we only had hand tools no power band saws that you see today. I had my own block and had to buy my own set of knives. Each block had a cleaver and large hand saw. But each piece was cut by hand.

From simple cuts like lamb chops and pork chops, he gradually worked me up to the most difficult cut of all - the huge round steak. This cut is from the large part of the hind leg and measures about 15 by 18 inches with a small round bone at one end. Usually the cut is thin, no more than half inch and the cut must be uniform through whole steak. This was done with the largest knife, about 15 inches long and several inches wide. It had to be very sharp to make even cuts. You start with the usual front to back stroke. When roughly half way through, you reverse the knife so the blade is pointed toward your elbow and proceed until you are past the bone. Then you cut the bone with the saw and finish the cut. Part of this steak is the top round and the smaller lower portion is the bottom round. These cuts are usually used for Swiss steak cooking. Very lean and somewhat tough. Also used for ground round. We always get ground chuck - for taste and juiciness.

Eventually Ray taught me how to break down the fore and hind quarters of a side of beef into the various roasts, steaks, and other cuts. The trimming from all these cuts and the less desirable parts ended up in hamburger. Lamb came in full carcasses and we had to split them in half and then break down each side. Arranging the display case was also part of the training. He took me with him to the packing houses and showed me how to select the best that was available. Even though I only weighed about 130 lbs I could carry a quarter of beef from the truck to a big swinging hook we used to break down the beef. Each quarter weighed about 150 to 175 lbs. He also taught me how to determine prices for each cut so a profit could be made. One of the useful skills he taught me was typing a knot around roasts that were rolled. It is a double half hitch, but you do it with one hand and when you pull it tight it snaps shut. I still use it to tie things together. He ran his business on a slim margin of about 17 percent..

Because he always had the highest quality and charged reasonable prices, we had customers from miles away. We were open from 8am to 6pm on Saturday and we had to be there at 7 and stay for cleanup at 7pm - a 12 hour day with hardly any time to sit or relax. We were busy all day. I even had my own customers who asked for me to wait on them each week. I remember this little lady Mrs. Rowe. She always bought a 2 inch thick porterhouse steak. Every Saturday she would wait for me and

I would say "Your steak Mrs. Rowe?" She would nod and I would get a loin of beef from the refrigerator and cut her steak. She bought other things but that part was routine.

Rationing started during the war and sometimes we couldn't get enough beef, lamb and pork. Once I was sent to another place to get and kill some chickens. There were about 150 of them and this place had a conveyor belt system. You hung the chickens by their feet from the conveyor which was over a long sink. I had to cut the chicken's throat and let it bleed into the sink. At the end of the conveyor belt was a tub of steaming hot water. You would dip the chicken in this tub and next to that was a large roller with rubber like fingers on the cylinder. After dipping the chicken in the water, you let the fingers on the roller take off the feathers. All done in a few seconds. I think I did all 150 chickens in about three hours. When I got back to the shop we had to gut all these chickens and then put them in the ice box. What a smelly job that was - feathers, blood and guts!

SAN LEANDRO HIGH SCHOOL

I worked at the market after school and on Saturdays and during summer vacation. All this was going on while in high school. We had three choices: college prep, industrial arts, or business. Naturally I opted for college prep not knowing if I would ever go to college. The high school was about 3 miles on the East side of town. I would ride my bike. During my senior year Ray let me drive his 1941 black convertible with red seats to school. Was I the envy of everybody.

The college prep curriculum allowed for few if any electives. I took Latin, English, History, science (biology, chemistry, and physics), and math (geometry, trig, analytical and solid geometry). We had two full semesters of trig and that really gave me a solid foundation for calculus and other high math I took in college. I had about 3-4 hours of homework every night. In those days everything was done by hand - no calculators or computers. There were typewriters but I never learned to type. My job provided me with all my spending money and I even bought most of my own clothes. My folks were never that well off. I didn't have time for sports though I was pretty good at baseball and football.

I was the friendly type much of it learned by waiting on people at the meat market. Even though I had only been at San Leandro for less than a year, I was elected student body secretary at the end of my sophomore year. Usually Juniors won that election but I gave a short speech patterned after the Gettysburg address and it won over the student body. My best friend was Dick Woodson. We were always together. He played on the football team and the golf team. With Dick and a half dozen other guys we founded a political party and ran that school for two years. We would win most of the elected positions and then we were able to appoint several other offices. We were always in the majority and really did some good things for the school. I was elected student body president even though I was in the hospital for appendicitis at the time.

Really enjoyed high school even though the academics were tough. We had good dedicated teachers and our class counselor Joe Bloom remained our friend for years after we graduated. I never went steady with anyone though Lois Griffith was the one I liked the best. Her father was a stock broker and I was from the blue collar part of town. She was a Christian Scientist and I was a Catholic so we knew nothing would ever develop but we were very good friends. Sometimes some of the guys and I would go over to Griff's house on Friday night just to socialize. Griff had 2 older sisters both of whom were quite attractive. Griff's Mom would always cook up a batch of Swedish pancakes. Boy were they good. We had dances and went to movies and the swimming pool and so forth. The Griffiths vacationed at Yosemite. One summer a few us went up there for a day and spent time with

them at their camp grounds. We were all just good friends and enjoyed each other's company.

I don't remember if I was the valedictorian but I had part in our graduation ceremony. **The class picture shows me smiling near the front center. Grif is 2 spots to the right.** of the group. San Leandro was always competitive in high school sports like football, baseball and basketball. We were the Pirates and our colors were blue and red.

During this time period the 1939 World's Fair was going on at Treasure Island. On one memorable visit, I ran along beside one of those slow moving trains and managed to talk with Loretta Young, Anita Louise and Don Ameche. Loretta was a doll and talked with me for a time. Anita looked on like she was interested but Ameche was a complete jerk looking like he was very bored. I always thought he was like that in his movies too. The picture at left is **Dede and Shirley Duffin** at the 1939 World's Fair. They look like movie stars, don't they?

CHAPTER VII - POST HIGH SCHOOL - THE UTAH CAPER

After graduating from high school, I continued to work at the meat market. For a short time I worked for Caterpillar Tractor Company as a machinist apprentice. I was just marking time before I went into the service since the war was going on. I learned a great lesson at CAT when I was assigned to drill some holes in a fuel injector piece. It was quite simple. You placed the small cylinder in a jig then you pulled down the drill arm three times. Each time you raised the arm the piece would rotate 120 degrees. So I was rolling along for about an hour when the bull of the woods (the shop foreman) came over and told me to slow down as I had already produced a day's output. You now know why things cost so much when you limit what labor can do.

About this time, **Bob Abrott** suggested that we see a little of the good old USA before Uncle Sam called. Over a period of several weeks, I took some of my clothes over to his house in preparation for

our adventure. Bob managed to "borrow" his grandmother's car and we took off one morning. I left a note for Mom and Dad with an admonishment "not to worry" and that we would let them know where we were.

We headed East through Nevada. At one stop in Nevada we had breakfast. One of the best I ever had. This was a really rough pit stop with a long wooden table and benches on each side. The food was brought out on serving trays with every breakfast food you could think of. You just helped yourself and ate till full. All for a buck. We arrived in Salt Lake with not many dollars left. I think we started with about $40 between us. When we arrived in Salt Lake one of the car tires was about to fail and during the war it was almost impossible to buy any. We asked around and were told that we could probably find work in Provo as they were building a big plant there.

We managed to make it to Provo and needed a place to stay. As we drove down a street, we saw a young man working in his yard. We stopped and asked him if he knew of any place we could find a room. He said "Wait a minute and I'll ask my mom". She came out and looked us over and decided we were OK and then stated "If you help clean up our back room, you can stay here."

We agreed on the princely sum of $5 per week for room and board and were set for about two weeks with what money we had left. Mrs. Gay was a great cook. She even baked her own bread. She was the widow of a railroad worker and she was a Mormon. They did not smoke or drink not even coffee. But she could swear like a boatswain's mate.

Within a few days we were hired at the new plant under construction as 4th year apprentice carpenters. Supposedly we had four years of prior experience. Manpower was scarce but it seemed strange that they would hire us like that when we obviously had no experience. I soon found out why.

My first day on the job the foreman gave me a stake and told me to drive it into the ground. I asked "Where do you want it?" He replied "Right where you are is OK". So I hammered the stake into the ground in a matter of seconds. I stood around for a few minutes until he returned. He said "Good job, Jack, now take it out and do it again." That is all I did all day - drive it in and take it out. Some time later I found out what a cost plus job was and that they were making a profit on what I was paid even if I did not do anything constructive. I was then assigned to a crew and we were building forms for foundations.

After a few weeks of this, I stumbled on a grocery store that had a meat market with no butcher. It was a real mess with dirty counters and rotten meat. I told the owner I was a journeyman meat cutter and was hired on the spot. I was paid about the same as the construction job but it was nicer indoors. I ran that market for about 4 months until Mom called me and told me I had to report for my induction physical. Bob in the meantime had found a job driving for a local trucking company. I went back to California on a bus. Bob stayed in Provo for about a year. He even attended BYU for a semester. I don't think Bob ever went into service because of some medical problem.

I returned to San Leandro about May 1943. I was sworn into the Navy with a reporting date of November 1943. So with time on my hands, I went looking for work. Remember that 60 acre field across the street from 285? Lo and behold, a developer was building houses there. So here I was with a 4th year carpenter apprentice union card (now an expert at driving stakes into the ground but little else) and was hired on the spot. **Dad/Jack '43**

My first day on the job was almost my last. I was an apprentice so I was a helper. One of the first things that happened was a carpenter asked me to get him a load of studs. Studs? What is a stud? Lucky for me they were desperate for any kind of help and Cecil, the foreman, had a great sense of humor. I was a willing worker and I kept my eyes and ears open. I learned rapidly and soon was doing 4th year apprentice work. From foundations to walls to roofing and finally even finish work. I worked on about 60 houses before I finally had to leave. For a few weeks my Dad even worked part time for them and we were assigned as a team. He was my helper though he was much better at most things than I was.

In 1999 Dede wrote the following poem that summarizes these first chapters.

MEMORIES

Do you remember when we were kids
pondering "eternity" just blew our lids
We'd scream and tear our hair
Not sure at all we'd want to go there

Now that you're still alive at 75
And I at 77 feel closer to heaven
I thought a brief review
of the lives of me and you
Would be a fun thing to do.

I see by a picture of two
I seemed to resent the likes of you,
but soon I was a mother hen
protecting you again and again.

But more than once you tried to drown
also pulling me down and down.
Who rescued us I don't recall.
Do you remember this at all?

I'm in the dark, but one was at Peninsula Park
The other at Farrelly Pool where we tried to keep cool.
So from the city of Roses and the snow
to the town of cherries we would go
at St.Mary's Avenue was the street
and it couldn't be beat
'cause we shared with our next of kin
ten cousins nearby (it makes you grin)

From St.Mary's Avenue to St.Mary's school
along the creek bed was pretty cool
Later when we were no longer tykes
We would go to school on our bikes.

We met the Bradows when Dad became a cop
and our friendship with their kids would never stop
What great friends we had with Shirley and Allan lad
Shirley and I with our paper dolls
and all of us as gangster and molls
Playing with our dogs and kitties
and building miniature cities

Riding bikes, and playing ball
any ol' time at all
how did "one foot across the gutter" go?
I don't remember, do you know?

listening to radio shows,
Jack Benny and Fred Allen were foes
There were spooky ones on Friday nites
Giving us more than our share of frights
Making us sure that in our attic
lurked a monster or a ghost?
Which scared us the most?

Later on, for Rick, Gary and Ron
This creature moved on
to the cellar, a most mysterious feller
Somehow he resembled Dad, it couldn't be all that bad.

If we weren't playing cards, to the movies we'd go
to the Palace Theatre to see a good show,
plus a newsreel, coming attractions and a B-movie.
Now I ask you what could be more groovy?

So for all of a dime we'd have a great time.
Movies were innocent in the thirties
firmly censored any of the dirties.

You might suspect we'd neglect our schooling,
but we got it all done, and I'm not fooling.
Our report cards are here to substantiate my claims
please note the A's and B's under our names!

Then we were there, at the World's Fair
and we actually saw and spoke to some Hollywood folk
like Loretta Young and Ty Power
Judy Garland actually gave me a flower

Besides the exhibits from foreign lands
we could actually dance to the Big Bands

Eventually we had to go our separate ways
as into the future we did gaze
You to Annapolis and I to the skies
Not knowing what before us lies

But we can't deny, it is no lie
God's been with us all the time
Not to thank Him would be a crime
On this we are of one accord,
So Deo Gratias, thank you Lord!

CHAPTER VIII - NAVY V12 AND UNIVERSITY OF CALIFORNIA

Before I graduated from high school, Dad asked me if I would like to go to the Naval Academy. Sounded good to me, though I did not know anything about the Academy. Dad had some good connections. You remember Judge Bruner? Well Dad as a police officer was on the Alameda County Kidnap Squad that was started soon after the Lindbergh kidnapping episode. The DA for Alameda County was Earl Warren. At this time he was Attorney General for California and later would become Governor and finally Supreme Court Justice. They wrote nice letters to our Congressman Carter and I received a first alternate for the 1943 entering class. When I was a LCDR I was able to visit Warren in Washington. His office room was enormous. It was like visiting the Wizard of Oz. It seemed like forever to cross that room on a very plush carpet to get to his desk. We talked for about 20 minutes about my Dad, San Leandro and family. He was very friendly and grandfatherly. It's too bad that the Warren Court left such a liberal legacy. He seemed like such a nice guy.

In preparation for the Naval Academy exams I attended Drew Prep School in San Francisco for several months. This school was devoted to preparing candidates for West Point and Annapolis. It was a very intense two months or so for me on Math and English. We worked hard and lived at the school. In two months we covered 4 years of high school math. We had fun riding the cable cars and going to downtown San Fran every Friday night. While there I met many men who eventually ended up at the Point or at USNA. This school helped me pass the exams with flying colors. While there we all took the Navy V12 exams which later proved to be important for me. The principle appointee apparently made it to the academy and that was that for 1943.

I enlisted in the Navy in May 1943 and due to those V12 exams I was slated for the **November 43** class **at Cal**. This was really nice since Berkeley was not far from San Leandro. Cal was on the quarter system since classes started in November. We were housed in Callahan Hall, the old international student quarters. I didn't find the academics too tough and enjoyed Cal. Reveille was at 6 a.m. We had about 30 minutes of calisthenics, then chow, then off to classes. About three times a week we had close order drill. **In this picture I am helping some of the guys with math.**

About twice a week the morning exercises was a run around the Campanile (Clock tower) which was about a mile and half run. One of the funny things that happened there was based on this. One morning a man got up about 3 am to go to the john. His roommate awoke after he left the room. His first reaction was that he missed reveille and the run. He threw on his clothes and rushed outside to catch up. He ran around the Campanile as the clock tower struck 3. He had missed nothing.

During one of our close order drills, a man broke ranks and began chasing some seagulls across the drill field. He was waving his rifle back and forth and cursing the poor seagulls. We never saw that man again.

My history prof at Cal was a very interesting and entertaining instructor. These classes were held in huge auditoriums with about 500 students. Yet this prof within a few weeks knew the names of every student in that class. Some ten years or more later I ran into him in New York and he still remembered my name. He was phenomenal.

When I returned from Utah, I met a lovely young lady, Mary Louise Donovan. We began to go steady then and while I was at Cal. It was really nice to be in the service and yet close enough to date one's home town gal. I was really in love with her and thought that some day we might get married. Silly me. There was a war going on and I would shortly be gone for a year. After my first year at USNA, we still dated that summer but shortly after returning to Annapolis in 45 I received my "Dear Jack" letter. It is interesting to know that we both had eight kids. Would we have had 16 if we had married? Perish the thought.

During this year at Cal I again asked Congressman Carter for an appointment to USNA. By this time he had received several letters from Earl Warren, then Governor of California, so again he made me a first alternate. At that point, I gave up on Annapolis and applied for civil engineering. I was slated to go to Case Institute where most civil engineers went for the Navy. As I was getting ready to go to Cleveland and Case, I was told that I had an appointment to Annapolis. Either the principle candidate failed his physical or Carter found another appointment. Anyway I was routed through Annapolis. If I could pass the physical there I would be transferred from USNR to USN. Everything else was in place.

I left Cal about a week before the end of the semester but was given credit for the courses I was taking. I took the train to Washington D.C. via Chicago. That was the worst trip I ever made. The cars were full of servicemen. There was no place to sleep. We eventually took the backs off of the seats and laid everything horizontal. When I arrived in Chicago I was filthy with dust, dirt and even soot. Managed to take a shower and get a little cleaned up there then off to D.C. Took a bus from there to Annapolis.

CHAPTER IX -- CANOE U -- THE NAVAL ACADEMY (1944-1947)

Arrived at USNA about 17 June and was directed to the crew ship the old Spanish Reina Mercedes that was moored at the far end of the Academy pier. Several days later I had to take the physical. I was worried because they are really tough. I think I only weighed about 135. So even though I passed several prior exams for the academy, I was not too confident about this one. If I failed, I would have gone on to Case Institute. Well I did obviously pass but the medics had quite a long discussion about my slight overbite. It's ironic because if I had gone to Case I would have been commissioned a year earlier and I eventually ended up in the Civil Engineer Corps anyway.

So I left the Reina and went to Bancroft Hall where we were issued all our gear. My roommate for plebe summer was Bud Lally from Louisville, Kentucky. He was a delight and we got along just fine. He bragged about Kentucky's fast horses and beautiful women and vise versa. Those first few days were real hectic - organizing all our uniforms, stenciling, spit polishing our shoes. Then the several months of pure boot camp - marching, shooting, rowing, and other drills from 6 a.m. until almost 6 at night. Bud and I would stand in front of the mirror with our officer caps on and wish for the day when we could wear them officially. Otherwise we wore sailor type gear all the time. There were trips to the tailor shop to be measured for our blues and whites and so forth. We were issued these only a few weeks before we joined the rest of the brigade and had to spend much time getting the fuzz off the dress blues. The picture above is **Bud and me in Haiti during first cruise.**

At the end of plebe summer, when the upper class returned we were assigned to our regular companies. I went to the 18th, the prior year color company, and Bud went to the first battalion, I think. Of course we saw each other for the next three years but it is different when you are not in the same company. We were introduced to our first classman (sort of a big brother) and mine was Hoot Gibson, a former Marine. Great guy and a big help to me. Plebe year is a sort of prolonged boot camp but not as intense. Plebes must be seen and not heard, must walk in the center of all corridors, must make square corners and eat square meals, must always keep "eyes in the boat" i.e. look straight ahead. At meals you must be prepared to answer questions posed by the upper class, many of them from the Plebe Manual. If you are unable to answer correctly, you are "shoved out" i.e. must eat sitting down without benefit of a chair. Or you may be told to hold out a pitcher of milk until your arm almost drops off. Meals only last about 20 minutes and plebes are last to be served. You learn to eat fast or starve. It is amazing how fast you can learn. If you really goof off, you are commanded to "come around" to the upper classman's room after meals. There you are required to do pushups equal to your class year - in our case 48. Most of this harassment is administered by the "Youngsters" the 3rd class. Those who just recently escaped all this. We had one little jerk who was the worst of the lot. The first and second classmen did not bother with much except the technical questions.

Sounds awful, but it was not that bad. I wasn't hassled too much. They usually picked on the real goof offs. If you got any demerits for talking in rank or a messy room you got a 15 and 4. That was fifteen demerits and 4 hours of extra duty. The extra duty was rowing boats in the river, butts manual, or marching alone. The yearly quota of demerits was 200. More than that and you could be booted out.

Each company group took the same subjects at the same time so we marched to class together. The officer of the day roamed about the yard as the mids marched to and from class. If he saw any infraction in a group, he would vector his plebe messenger to put the culprit on report. Sometimes this officer would hide behind the bandstand like a traffic cop. If another group saw this and were far enough away to be safe they would sing out "Sail Ho behind the bandstand" to warn approaching groups. One time when we arrived at the terrace level near Bancroft Hall, someone thought he saw a vectored plebe approaching. He yelled out a warning and we all scattered like a covey of quail. There was no messenger around.

On unique feature at the Academy was a daily quiz in every subject. Each day's quiz was graded and become part of the semester grade. This method insured that you always kept up with the work. Most of the time the quiz work was done on the blackboards and each midshipman had a different question or problem to work on. As you entered the classroom, the instructor would command **"Gentlemen, man the boards."**

Fall was great because of the football games - some of which we went to by train or boat. We always went to Philly for the Army game. Marching into that stadium in front of 60,000 people was always a thrill. If Navy beat Army the pressure was off the plebes for the rest of the year.

We lost to Army every year I was there. The 46 game is still considered the best Army-Navy game of all time. With Blanchard and Davis Army was the National Champ and Navy had lost most of its games. But we almost beat them losing 21 to 18 when we were on the Army 4 yard line. One of the interesting side lights of the game is a play Army used that we on the 150 lb team knew very well. The week before this Army game the lightweights ran the Army pass plays against the varsity. I was "Davis" for these plays. On this play it looks like Blanchard is running to the left, but he stops and passes to Davis who had drifted out to the left side. We ran that play successfully many times and I always scored a TD with it. As I watched from the stands I saw this play develop and I hid my face. Again it was successful but Army did not score with it. After the away games we always found a party somewhere to go to. Then we had to get back to the ferry or train about midnight for the trip back to Annapolis.

As a plebe you could not "drag" (date a girl). We would stand in the balcony of the armory and watch the dancing below. It was always a great sight to see the dress blues or whites and the girls in their formals. For the plebes there would be tea dances on Sunday afternoon with some of the local "belles". I rarely went to those functions. It made you feel like a little kid at his first dance.

On Christmas leave there was not enough time to go West so I spent the first year in upstate New York with one of my roommates. The second year I spent with Dede also in New York. The third year I went to Johnny Wick's house in D.C.

After Christmas came the "dark ages". Bad weather, not much in athletics, and just academic work. Also every semester, each mid had to participate in some athletic endeavor from 4 to 6 p.m. First year I boxed on the company team (never lost) and battalion lacrosse. Second year did military track and lacrosse. Last year was 150lb football (lettered and we won Eastern Crown), and battalion lacrosse. This was the first year that the Academy had entered a 150lb football team in this competition. It was really fun because there was no one on the field that weighed more than 154lbs. I was at 150 exactly. Played both ways - free safety on defense and half back on offense. We played Princeton for our first game and they were the champs from the prior year. We won easily 19-0 and I managed to intercept 3 passes. Had 7 for the season. The only close game was against Rutgers and we barely won with a field goal. The last game against Pennsylvania was a slaughter 45-6. They scored first and got us mad. I scored my only touchdown that game with a side line pass and a 45 yd run. The interesting thing about that run was that I was running down the right side line. All they had to do was push me out of bounds. But I faked to the right and broke left and managed to butt my head into the end zone. A couple of Penn players came up to me after the game and said that it was the best run they had seen that year..

Finally Spring and June week. June week is something else at USNA. There are all kinds of proms and outdoor activity and finally the graduation of the first class. Immediately after that, the plebes scale up a greased up Herndon Monument. When a cap is placed on the top, the plebes graduate to third class and all that harassment is over. In 1945 the war was almost over and the academy had to go back to a four year program from the 3 year program. Our class was split academically into 48A and 48B. 48A was to finish in 3 years and 48B in four. I stood 56th out of 1000, so I was in 48A and was a second classman without ever being in third class. Neat to have those **two stripes instead of one.** Because of the split, we were all sent to different companies and some of the 18th ended in the 11th my final company. One other event happened plebe year that you may be able to see from time to time on the History Channel. The 5th Battalion was chosen to march in the funeral procession for President Roosevelt. I have seen that parade on TV several times and there we are.

Spent a month at home in '45. Enjoyed it very much. I was promised an airplane ride back to Washington from Alameda Air Station. The Admiral changed his mind at the last moment and I had to take the train. Ended up two days late at Annapolis and that got me a class A offense. The Commandant said he had to make an example of me and gave me 100 demerits and six weeks in hack. So I only had 100 demerits to play with for the year but the "in hack" was the worst. During the academic summer, I had to report every half hour to the Battalion or Main office, the Main office on the hour when I was not in class. Gets pretty hard for six weeks. Then off for summer cruise.

During plebe summer we had a short cruise in Chesapeake Bay on LSTs. We went through some landings like marines, ate the K rations and so forth. During that cruise some hot shot pilot buzzed our ships and made a fatal error. He got too low and his right wing clipped the bow of the ship in front of ours. The plane did a slow roll and disappeared below the water in seconds. Three classmates were killed in the incident. We later found out that the pilot had his girl friend in the plane. They also were both killed.

Second class summer we cruised on the USS Marblehead, an old four stack cruiser. We went through all the departments; engine room; CIC; bridge, and gunnery. I was the center trayman in one of the main 6" batteries. I stood between the two guns and when we loaded the shells and powder, I first rammed the two trays into the breeches of the guns. When the guns fired, the guns recoiled back past where I was standing. Exciting, I can tell you! We were berthed in a compartment right between the stacks and right above the ship's bakery. From time to time, we were able to snitch some baked goods by reaching through the port hole as we went up the outside ladder.

It was an interesting cruise. We were the first U.S. ship to stop at Haiti since before the war. We also stopped at St. Thomas and Cuba. We did some shore bombardment down there. We also stopped at Fall River in Massachusetts. All in all it was fun.

My first class cruise was on the **USS Washington BB61.** My battle station was in CIC (Combat Information Center) where we actually pulled the triggers for the 16" guns. Our team won the award for the best that summer. It was interesting watching the progress of a 16" broadside on our radar screen as the projectiles traveled some 15 plus miles to the target. During the six weeks of academics we had during the summer, I was a 4 striper, Battalion Commander. Except for a silly event on the Washington, I probably would have been a 4 striper or more that year since my "grease" was high in my class - somewhere near the top ten. The term "grease" refers to marks each Mid received for aptitude for the service. My grade was 3.9 most of the time.

The silly event occurred near the end of the Washington cruise. Ben Conroy, Falevsky and I were goofing off in a 20mm gun enclosure when some fat LTjg found us and put us on report. So my "grease" suffered and I only ended up my senior year as a 2 striper on the regimental staff. This never really bothered me as such rankings at the academy had little effect on the big picture. Academics were the really important part of life at old Canoe U and I did OK there. My plebe year I stood 56 out of 1000. Once I got rid of such things as history, English, and foreign languages and had subjects that were mostly math oriented, my class standing steadily improved. Second class year I stood 37th out of 500 and first class year I zoomed to 6th. I was first in Navigation and close to the top in gunnery and steam (Thermodynamics). My final graduation standing was 14 out of the 500.

You must realize that back in those days we did not have the benefit of calculators or computers. We had to use log tables or slide rules for math related problems. Every Saturday morning first class year we had a P work. This was a four hour Navigation problem. You started with a chart and a ship's position and then during the next four hours using provided star sights, current data and land sightings you plotted your ship's progress. You could never complete the problem but only go as far as time permitted. The more accurate you worked and the faster you worked the better. I did not try to rush through the problem but worked with care - cross checking every calculation. As I remember it, I never made a single error that whole year and as a result, I placed first in Navigation.

We also had a lot of actual sea drills on YPs. These were small 2 engine cabin cruisers that we used in Chesapeake Bay. We would work with 3 other boats for various drills and simulated attacks and so forth. Lots of fun and very educational. We also had a CIC simulator that was very realistic. There we could plot and make torpedo runs or fire salvos at radar targets. First class year really prepared us for the fleet with gunnery, navigation, seamanship, and engineering. When we graduated and joined the fleet we were ready to do most any job assigned to us. A sad story concerns one first classman in these CIC drills. They are very realistic and also very stressful. During one of these drills this mid got so excited that he began to stutter and could not give the order to fire the torpedoes. He graduated but was not commissioned. Bud was also not commissioned due to poor eyesight.

UNCLE BEANY JARRETT

Before I leave old USNA I must relate a few stories about a really fabulous character who later played an important role in my life in the Navy. When I was a plebe, I was in the fifth battalion. We had to learn a song about the previous battalion officer a Commander Jarrett. The song was titled "Uncle Beany is our guide". Later we learned about some of his escapades as a USNA watch officer. He was loved by all who knew him because of his sense of humor and leadership. A few stories should give you a sense of this man.

The dining hall in Bancroft Hall could seat the entire brigade at one sitting, some 4000 men. It seems to extend forever when you first see it. Each table had about 16 to 18 men at it with a combination of all 4 classes. The first classmen sat at the ends and the plebes were in the middle, with the 3rd and 2nd classmen on the sides. Regulations forbid anyone taking food from the dinning hall. Naturally, only the first class dared to violate this regulation. They were finished eating first since they were served first. Sometimes they left before we had all finished eating. Since most officers ate with the mids and stayed until the meal was finished, this provided an opportunity to take some food, mostly desserts, from the dinning hall.

As the story goes, one first classman was taking a full cake from the dinning hall when he runs into Commander Jarrett who had the duty that day. When you have the duty, you wear your sword as he did. As he was being placed on report, the first classman pleaded with Jarrett, "Gee, Commander, since you are putting me on report can't I at least have the cake?". The cake at this time was being held by the midshipman messenger. Jarrett hesitated a few seconds then drew out his sword and cut the cake in half. He gave half to the firsty and took the other half for himself.

Between the wings of Bancroft Hall is a nice area of trees, benches, flowers and so forth called Smoke Park. One early evening CDR Jarrett, again on duty, was walking around Smoke Park when he found a first classman making out with one of the girls who worked in the Academy laundry. This was rather embarrassing for all concerned. This was a Class A offense one meriting dismissal from the Academy. So Uncle Beany told the midshipman to put himself on report and bring the report to him at the main office. This was a disaster for the midshipman since there was only a month to go before graduation. Knowing that CDR Jarrett had a sense of humor and that he had virtually nothing to lose, the midshipman desperately reviewed the reg book seeking some remedy. At last he made out the report and took it to CDR Jarrett at the main office. Standing stiffly at attention, the mid kept his eyes in the boat and waited for Jarett's response. After reading the report for a few minutes, Jarrett finally smiled, signed the report and dismissed the mid. The mid did not receive a Class A offense and graduated with his class. CDR Jarrett must have thought that the mid had learned his lesson and that he would make a good officer since he showed a great deal of creativity. What did he do? The report he had submitted was only a 5 demerit offense without even some extra duty. The offense reported was "Laundry bag, unauthorized articles in".

How did Jarrett have an impact on my career? He was the commanding officer of my first ship the USS Astoria CL90. More on that later.

DAILY LIFE AT USNA

The daily routine was very military. Reveille was at 6 a.m.; breakfast formation at 6:30. March to breakfast (we always marched to everything); breakfast was about 25 minutes long; back to rooms to get ready for first class. March to class; march back etc. all day long. From 4 to 6 was for sports. Everyone had to participate in some form of organized sports everyday. From varsity, jv, battalion, or company. I played lacrosse, boxed, flag football, military track, gymnastics, and senior year 150lb varsity football.

Three things each mid had to accomplish. Pass the strength test, the swimming test, and the military obstacle course. The last was easy for me since it was the same course used in military track. I could do that obstacle course in roughly half the time allowed. We had a man in our class of the Chicago Palmers - very wealthy and owner of the Palmer House in Chicago. This poor guy was on the weak squad, the swimming squad, and the obstacle squad. Each year the qualifications for these three requirements was tougher and he would barely pass each year but could not meet the next years goals.

So he never was able to participate in any other sports but had to work on the strength, swimming and obstacle course every week for all the years he was there.

Palmer was so off the ball, that his midshipman company commander sent him on a world cruise. There are about 250 tables in the mess hall. A world cruise requires the plebe to visit a new table every night until he completes the entire circuit, the world cruise. He must perform some feat at each table and carry a log book of his trip. Palmer was required to learn the commands required to bring a three mast ship about, that is change from port to starboard tack or vis versa. When he arrived at each new table, the senior first classman would look at the log and then as the meal ended he would command "Mr. Palmer, bring the ship to the starboard tack".

There are about 15 or 20 commands required and it takes about 5 minutes to complete the task. The first command "Standby to come about" would bring complete silence to the entire mess hall. Palmer did have a commanding and loud voice. He did not need any loud speaker assistance. Then he would recite all the commands and finally the last "Sir, the ship is on the starboard tack!" would ring out. The entire brigade would give him a rousing cheer for this performance. He was really outstanding.

Another unique custom at USNA was called the **"bricking party"**. If a mid dragged a girl who was  not quite a Dallas Cheerleader type, he would experience a Sunday night bricking party. 15 or more of his classmates would gather in his room all dressed in ridiculous costumes. They would serenade the poor guy with songs like "If you knew Suzy" and then present him with a red brick on a pillow. Invariably the mid would exclaim "But she had a great personality."

Every week the Brigade would assemble on the drill field for various situations and for various dignitaries. After all that we would pass in review. Six battalions, 24 companies, would then march to the right, make two left turns and pass the reviewing stands. We were in dress blues or blue jackets with white pants and it really was an impressive show. I can still remember the visiting college and high school girls gushing over all those good looking young men. The various regimental and battalion staffs had a spectacular turning method. Precise and swift - really neat. Bayonets and swords flashing in the sun to the marine bands Sousa music. My feet still can't keep still when I hear that music.

DEDE VISITS USNA - SPRING 1946

Dede made a visit to Crab Town in the Spring of 46 and she wrote it up. She captures the Academy and Annapolis quite well so let me just quote from her letter.

"Hit the picturesque Academy town at 7 a.m. exactly just in time to watch the boys march to St. Mary's for Sunday Mass. Bud met me there to tell me in a woebegone manner that Jack had the 10 o'-clock church party instead of the seven. I rec'd communion and felt very happy to be receiving the

Host with a whole line of midshipmen at the rail. Took a little nap after breakfast in Carvel Hall and then met Jack for the later Mass. When he marched back to the Academy I trotted along after them to take snaps --- the boy leading the lot said "Company, halt!" and they stood there while I took a picture. Jack said out of order, "Don't say we aren't gentlemen." I got a big kick our of it --- and so did the boys. At the Main Gate met Jack at 11:30 and I went hog wild taking pictures... took one of the Protestant boys and their dates gathered around the Chapel. Then Jack showed me thru the Chapel--- then we walked over to the harbor—we both love that old salty smell. Next he had to leave me again for a few minutes for formation. To the boom boom of drums and trumpets the boys marched into Bancroft Hall. Their precision is as beautiful as you see in the movies—truly a stirring sight. I ate it up. Next with another couple we gave the first classmen ten minutes grace for the chow houses and then set out ourselves for our noonday repast. We had a nice meal in an atmospheric little place called the Blue Lantern spiced with the boys amusing imitations of their profs...from what the boys say, those teachers know next to nothing about the subject they profess to convey. For example, one prof comes into the room, announces "I'm a math teacher, I don't know anything about juice." Juice (electricity) is the subject he's supposed to be teaching, great, huh? And the nick names they have for these fellows, it's a riot. Here are some of those names: 'Hot Lead Eddie'; 'The Sneaking Deacon'; 'Rodger the Lodger'; 'Dumbo Wilson'; 'Black Jack Hammond'; 'Shaky Lee'.

Jack showed me thru the gym and along the athletic grounds. My feet were killing me about this time (I mean it) and I collapsed in a park behind Bancroft Hall and we talked awhile. Next Jake showed me the mess hall, biggest in the world, by which I was duly impressed. Looks like San Quentin's chow room, the difference being Jack says are the dishes aren't tin, but THAT'S THE ONLY DIFFERENCE!

There was an informal dance, juke box variety in Bancroft Hall so we next tripped the light fantastic---Jack dances very well, but then look who taught him! Played ping pong too---and then my feet still hurting, we sat out most of the dances and criticized the characters on the floor. I gave Jack a lesson on colors, chartreuse, turquoise, apple green, cerise, etc.—but he got too sharp after awhile, noticing slight variations in shade, etc. and asking me what that was—it would invariably be some shade I'd already pointed out and yet not be quite the same tone as the first example. And the most wonderful part of all I convinced Jake I was the best person in the world **he should ask for June Week** and so it's all settled. I'm really all hepped up about the subject. We can have a lot of fun. (It was and we did).

Jack's got such a wonderful sense of humor and old lady LeDoux feels so much younger among all those "kids". (Note: she was only a year older than many of the mids).

Next we had a sundae and Jack saw me off on the bus. He looks mighty good, as usual, and you'll be surprised at how straight his teeth now are. (Note: they slipped back after some time).

This is for you Jack...I guess you realized that I really enjoyed that Sunday more than I can say. It somehow meant an awful lot to me and I was very happy that I had the inspiration to see that day. I thot about it all the way home." End of Dede's tale.

JUNE WEEK

Plebe June week was remembered mostly for turning from plebes to upper classmen. Home for my first visit in a year. June Week 46 was great because that was when we got our rings and went to the Ring Dance. I "dragged" quite a bit mostly with blind dates since I was from California. **Dede was my date for our Ring Dance** and it was really special. She was very attractive - TWA hostess and all and many of my friends in the first class wanted to meet her. We dipped our rings in water from the seven seas and then became the almighty first classmen with all the privileges thereto. It is hard to imagine the difference between that and merely being a senior at a civilian school. June week 47 and graduation was something else. Senior prom, the N Dance, the various parades and boat trips. Mom and Dad were there. My date Bobby Ballou was also there. Forrestal (the first Secretary of Defense) was our graduation speaker and his message "You face an uncertain world" was certainly true. We were somewhat disappointed that there was no war to fight. We wanted to put all our skills to use. Little did we know that only a few years later we would have that war and a number of my classmates were killed in Korea.

So the supreme moment finally arrived and we **threw our caps in the air** with a tremendous cheer. Those middy caps became someone's souvenir - never got mine back. We went outside and Mom and Bobby put on my new ensign shoulder boards and I was, at last, an ensign in the U.S. Navy with orders for a light cruiser, the USS Astoria CL90.

We said our farewells to our classmates with resolve to see each other sometime. Most I have never seen again - only Ben, Ski, Mac and Bob have I ever seen more than a few times. Ben Conroy became a cable TV pioneer; Ski became president of Smith Steel Company; Mac became a 2 star admiral, and Bob Bonnell an insurance exec. Sam Pennock ran his family florist business in Philadelphia. Mike, Duffy's partner told me that the Pennock's were the largest florists in the United States. I saw my roommate only once when John Wick got married in New Jersey in 1950. I was his best man. In 1951 Johnny's weather plane disappeared somewhere in the Bermuda Triangle. No trace was ever found of the plane. Somewhere in the Naval Academy stadium is a seat bearing his name. It was the least I could do for such a great guy.

We packed all my gear in the 41 chevy and took a long trip through Michigan and the northern states. Saw a couple of Dad's sisters whom he had not seen for many years. It was really fun. Went through northern Idaho on a dirt road that had a US highway marker on it. Even had to ford a creek on that road. Stopped in Portland and visited the family there. Finally arrived home in San Leandro and had several weeks before I had to report to the Astoria. This is last **photo of the 11th** company before graduation.

Fall 1946 - Regimental Staff - Jack top left

CHAPTER X - USS ASTORIA CL90 (1947-1948)

My first ship was the light cruiser USS ASTORIA CL90. We called her the Gay 90. Imagine what that phrase would cause today! At USNA we had a lottery to determine ship preference. I wanted a cruiser and a West Coast ship and my lottery number was low enough so I got what I wanted. I even asked for the ASTORIA because I heard she was a good ship. For those who are curious, the difference between a light and heavy cruiser was her main battery. The light cruiser had 6 inch guns and the heavy had 8 inch main battery. Otherwise they were very much the same. Our squadron consisted of the USS Helena (flagship) and the USS Springfield.

My orders sent me to Seattle where the ASTORIA was supposed to be. I went by train and she was not in Seattle. I was then sent to San Diego - again no ASTORIA. Finally it must have been through Naval Intelligence that she was located in Long Beach - in dry dock no less. She had been in dry dock for months and there I was trying to find a land locked ship. How did we win WWII?

As it turned out, my late arrival was of great benefit to me. All the other 5 new ensigns had been sent off to various fleet schools except me. I was assigned as division officer of the 5th Division. My battle station was the 5" control officer. The 5" batteries (there were six of them) were primarily for AA and shore bombardment. The 5" director was high above the bridge, about as high as you can get. Even though we had two directors, one fore and the other aft, we only had crew enough to man one. In fact we could only man half the 5" batteries at any one time. At the Academy I had spent many practice hours in a 5" director, so I felt right at home in my battle station.

I was also assigned to the sea detail as JOOD (Junior Officer of the Deck). That meant that anytime we left or came into port, I was on the bridge. The OOD (Officer Of the Deck) is a key position when a ship is underway at sea. Next to the Captain and the Exec (the #2 officer) the OOD was in command of the ship. Later you will see how that affected me. All of these things were not really new to me since the trade school (USNA) in those days did prepare you to be an effective officer on a ship.

The **ASTORIA** left dry dock soon after I came aboard and we went to sea for our sea trials. We only had about half of our complement aboard and as a result I went from a JOOD to an OOD within a few months. This was quite an honor since it usually took about a year to be qualified as an OOD. Several factors made this possible. One was the depleted size of our crew and other was the quick rotation of commanding officers. Every potential flag officer must command a capital ship at sea - a battleship, cruiser or an aircraft carrier. The COs only stayed aboard for about nine months.

Captain Jarrett was the CO when I arrived and I guess he took a liking to me and that's why I was made an OOD. Each Captain only qualified a few officers as OODs since they had to trust these men literally with their careers. If anything happened, the old man was always responsible. We had only 4 qualified OODs and at sea we rotated the watch at sea with those four men. The senior watch officer was a full LT, another LT Taylor and a LTjg and then me as an Ensign. I remember the story of the USS Missouri and her new Captain. He had just reported aboard and ship went to sea from the Chesapeake Bay. Somehow she ran aground and his career was over in about 2 hours after taking over. So you see these Captains had to be careful who was an OOD.

A few stories will illustrate life at sea. When I was still doing the JOOD thing we were at sea operating with a carrier Task Force. It was night and very dark. The carrier had turned into the wind to launch aircraft. Our ship had to maneuver to get into our normal relative position from the carrier. Destroyers were doing the same thing. It can get very confusing and things happen so fast. All of a sudden we were heading right at the carrier's starboard side. Captain Jarrett waited a few seconds for the OOD to do something but he seemed frozen. "Right full rudder, all back full" commanded the Captain. The ship heeled over and I could hear dishes breaking in the wardroom. We missed a collision by not much but old Uncle Beany was on the job. I don't remember what happened to that OOD but maybe that's why I got the opening.

We were getting ready to go to sea while tied up in San Diego. I was on the bridge looking over at the pier when a large rotund (shall I say) LCDR came up to me and asked me a question. "What are those called?" he asked pointing toward the pier. "What do you mean, sir?" I asked in return. "Those ropes" he replied. "Oh, you mean the lines that the ship is tied up with?". He nodded and I then named them from bow to stern "Forward spring line,...etc.". He thanked me and left and I thought to myself, 'Well we have another two week reserve officer aboard who has seldom if ever been on a ship. Later that day I discovered, to my horror, that this rotund officer, a Mr. Martin*, was our new navigator. I vowed to keep my eye on that officer and as you shall see he became one of my favorite sea stories. *Not real name.

Some time later we were operating with a carrier task force in practice maneuvers. I was the OOD. Capt Jarrett and Martin were also on the bridge. We were in a position on the port side of the carrier about 2000 yds astern. When the command came that the carrier was going to turn into the wind to launch aircraft we had to work out a maneuvering board problem to determine a course and speed for our ship to get into the same relative position once the carrier turned into the wind. We were going at fairly high speed (28 knots) as the carrier needed as much speed as possible to launch aircraft. You usually have several minutes to work out the problem.

I worked out my solution and Martin did one too. Before the execute command came over the radio, Jarrett looked at Martin and said "What is your solution Mr. Martin?". Martin gave out his course and speed and I could see Capt. Jarrett's eyebrows arch in a questioning manner. "LeDoux what is your recommendation?" Jarrett asked me. I told him my solution. Quietly the Captain said "Let's try LeDoux's". Martin left the bridge. Later on Mr. Martin had a maneuvering board school for all junior officers. I was specifically excused.

My favorite interaction with the great navigator occurred on another fleet exercise. We were again operating with a carrier and going through a number of exercises. The navigator was being a busy body on the bridge which is not that large a space. Capt Jarrett was on the starboard side and I on the port. Our rotund friend was occupying a great deal of space and really getting in the way. I finally ran out of patience and addressed him thus "Mr. Martin, do you want to relieve me?" He meekly replied "No, of course not." Said the Ensign to the LCDR, "Then please leave the bridge, Sir!" I glanced over at the Captain who had not uttered a word. I could see him smiling.   Martin left the bridge. I was always amazed that he continued to be very friendly with me. I thought he might be angry with such an upstart junior officer. He was 3 grades my senior.

The last story about Mr. Martin occurred when I was on the beach with our pistol team. The ship went to Alaska for two weeks and was entering the harbor at Juneau. The entrance was like a river and the ship had to make several turns. At the first turn the Captain (not Jarrett) asked Martin if it was time to turn. "Not yet" replied our great navigator. Finally the Captain's seaman's eye got the best of him. "Did you allow for advance and transfer?" asked the skipper in alarm. The blank look on Martin's face was answer enough. Another all back full and right full rudder was required. A ship does not turn on a dime. Because of inertia the ship travels (advances) in its original direction for hundreds of yards and as it turns it transfers additional yardage. You must know these characteristics which depend on the ship's speed to avoid running aground.

Our second skipper after Jarrett left was a very nervous man a Captain Hofheinz. I only remember one incident with him. I was the OOD again and we were operating independently. We had gone several hours with little change in speed or direction. As we approached Long Beach, we had to reduce speed from full to one-third ahead. On the bridge there is a device called the Engine Order Telegraph. It is about 4 feet high and has two arms sticking out from a round device that indicates the speed on the port and starboard engines. This device sends info to the engine room, and the engineers then take appropriate action. So I turn to the sailor on the Telegraph and ordered "All ahead one-third". A very simple order to follow. All the man had to do was move up from "Full" to the one-third position. The young sailor does nothing. I give the order again, this time rather sharply. The kid panics and moves the levers to all back full. "No, no!" I shout. He then moves them to the all ahead full position. The sailors hands have frozen to the handles as I try to take them off. The Captain jumps on one side and I on the other as we move the levers back and forth several times until we finally stopped on the correct position. We find out the kid had never been on a bridge before and had been sent up without any instructions by his petty officer. Later I asked the engineer what happened in the engine room with all these commands. He said "There were bells going off all over the place and I just had to wait until it settled down." That event certainly broke the boredom.

AA PRACTICE

My battle station was the 5" director, essentially for anti-aircraft fire or shore bombardment. There are three positions in this small steel container: the pointer (up and down), the trainer (left and right) and the director (me). When incoming aircraft are sighted by me, I had a joy stick that controlled the pod and I would sight on the planes. I would then send verbal info to CIC (Combat Information Center) with estimated plane speed, altitude and target angle. The pointer and trainer would pick up the plane and begin tracking it. All of this info was fed into CIC computers that would quickly determine real speed, altitude and angle and then aim the guns on the plane(s). All this would happen in a few seconds and then the guns would begin firing automatically as they were loaded by the gun crews. Each mount (there were six of them) could fire about 30 rounds per minute. With a full and well trained crew, the AA fire was quite deadly.

We did not have a full or well trained crew since the turnover after the war was severe. To improve our battle efficiency we had AA practice quite often when we were at sea. A plane would tow a sleeve and fly over the ship. We could fire only during short intervals so that we would not come close to the plane. A horn would blow when we could start firing and again when we must stop firing.

This one day as we prepared to practice with an undermanned crew I could hear over my ear phones the confusion in the gun mounts. The crews had to run from the port to the starboard guns depending on the plane's approach. As the first horn blew, I could hear the gun captain cursing his crew to get the guns loaded. Time passed quickly with no firing until the last horn sounded. As it sounded we were able to fire one shot. Remember these mounts can fire 30 rounds per minute. As the last horn sounded, LT Taylor the secondary gun boss, looked up at me and said "Is that the best that you can do?". I looked skyward and then said to Taylor, "That's all it takes sir". LT Taylor looked up to see the sleeve fluttering down toward the sea. We had luckily hit and severed the tow cable. He just smiled and shook his head.

Another time something got fouled up with CIC because we were firing at the sleeve but the flak was ending up in front of the plane. The pilot, in disgust, radioed "Hey you guys, I'm towing this thing not pushing it!".

It was a good thing that the war was over and we had won.

As you all know I have always been a people oriented kind of guy. I think I developed that attitude from my years working in the butcher shop and waiting on people. This attitude paid off because I took a real interest in all the enlisted men in my division. Spent the time and effort to get to know each man and helped him toward whatever goal he was seeking in the Navy. I had one of the first black sailors who was not a stewards' mate. He was an imposing man, tall and well built. He was sort of a Jackie Robinson for the Navy. He was an excellent sailor always impeccable in dress and deportment. As soon as he reported aboard, I was accosted by a committee of sailors, all from Southern States. They did not want a "nigger" sleeping in their compartment. "Well men" said I "I guess you will have to sleep out on deck because he stays in this division and he stays in the compartment". They looked at me in total shock not expecting that a white officer would not agree with them. Never heard another word about it and that black sailor was finally accepted for what he truly was - a good sailor and a fine man.

Another funny incident occurred in that division. The top enlisted man in my gunnery division was a boatswain's mate first class. I had one tough dude as my bos'n mate - 6ft 2" tall and strong. One of his many duties is to roust out the men at reveille. He had little patience with this chore. At quarters one morning I noticed that one of my men has a black eye. I asked him how he got it. "Ran into a stanchion, sir". The bos'n was right behind me, so I turned to him and said "Good morning, stanchion!". He just smiled a little grin. I was the only junior officer who got up at reveille with my men and was on deck with them during the work they did before breakfast. Uncle Beany complimented me on this. The end result was that my division was the best at inspection and drills.

One of the enlisted men I became friends with was Vernon Wilcox. At one point he had been a 1st class petty officer, one grade below chief but was now the ship's bugler, a seaman first class. He was not in my division but we spent many hours together in port watches. Especially during the night watches there is not much to do but shoot the breeze. We even spent several liberties together in civilian clothes, though this was not kosher. He thought enough of me to write a poem. See end of chapter.

Life on board a warship is fun if you learn to roll with the punches. After the ship was out of dry dock we went for a series of sea trials to make sure everything was shipshape. When we later joined our other cruisers in the squadron we were scheduled for a material inspection by the Admiral who had a very severe reputation. His nick name said it all - Herman the German. We knew we were in for it when he was first piped aboard and he barked at our skipper "One of your side boys shoes are not tied!"

Since we had only recently left the shipyard, there were still many things not completely organized. In one deck division, the bos'n had put a lot of last minute gear in a deck locker and put an enlisted man inside with instructions not to let anyone in. Murphy's law is always in effect during inspections and lo and behold Admiral Herman passed the locker, paused and ordered the master at arms to open the locker. Ship's watertight doors have a number of arm like levers around the perimeter of the door. As the master at arms began opening these levers, the man inside just as quickly closed them again. They went around twice until the Admiral roared in anger and the bos'n told his man to stop locking the door. Needless to say, that was a down check..

The final blow on that inspection was caused by an Ensign Dobson . He was near the bottom of his class. If ever there was a man that should not have graduated from Canoe U, he was that man. He had absolutely no common sense even though his father was a Captain in the Navy and also known for his temper. He said of his old man "He's a real SOB, isn't he?" Dobson was in communications and was in the radio room when he saw Admiral Herman pass by. He got on the intercom and in a loud voice was warning those in the Admiral's path "The big Brass in on his way!" Apparently the Admiral had paused and entered the radio room and was standing directly behind Dobson. "The big Brass is right here, son" he remarked in a loud voice. I really think that Herman enjoyed this inspection as much as those of us who hadn't screwed up.. **Officers Shore Party to the right.** We would lead the sailors if we had to land a party on the beach.

Little things are very important. During general quarters (battle stations) communications are made with sound powered phones. So one day I gave a brief lecture to my division on how to store these phones properly. If they are all tangled up delays would result getting ready for battle. So I asked one of the sailors to go get the nearest phone that are stored in small cabinets near gun mounts. The one

he brought me was a perfect example of what not to do. The crew thought that I had messed it up on purpose but I was innocent. So I showed them how to properly coil up the line. We all had a good laugh over this messed up phone. **This picture shows Uncle Beany leaving the Astoria.** Many years later I met him again at Bethesda Naval Hospital. We were both taking our annual physicals. We had a good time remembering what happened on the good ship Astoria. I really should have checked out those Naval Academy legends.

TO MY FRIEND - MR. LeDOUX

As long as I'm a seaman,
and have so little dough,
I have few ways to show you,
that you're my favorite Jo.

I know it's not acceptable,
to give a gift to you,
so I will write some poetry,
at least it's something new.

I'd like to press the fact to you,
that you're my most liked boss,
between the other "braid" aboard,
I believe it is a toss.

I hope that when my time is up,
I'll know you as my pal,
I want to come and visit you,
and meet your lovely gal.

So always think of me as one,
that gives you due regard,
and may we meet in later life,
to play in your back yard.

I know the poem is rather bad,
in spots it's kind of fair,
but anyway you get the point,
and see the thought that's there.

I'll go for now, and hope for you,
a life that'd full of cheer,
and may we cross our paths some day,
and share a nice cold beer.

Vernon was from San Francisco and I have never seen him again.

THE BLIND DATE

We junior officers lived in the JO bunk room. There were bunks for about a dozen officers but we only had six. Three of us were USNA grads from my class and three were from various ROTC units. My two classmates, Bill Bass and Hank Clay went on to interesting careers - Bill to work for Rickover and Hank to submarines. It was very crowded in the bunk room. We all had a bunk and two lockers to hold all our gear. The ROTC guys were Cleve and Kolar. Can't remember the third guy.

Cleve and Kolar were liberty friends. Bill and Hank were already married. So I buddied up with LTjg Jim Hayes. Jim played golf and dragged me out to Recreation Park one day. I think I broke 100 that first time and had a few pars so that's when the golf bug bit me. As bachelors on liberty we visited the local watering holes in San Diego and Long Beach. Nothing ever happened aside from drinking a beer or two. Sometimes I would go bowling. There was a hotel on the beach with a lounge on the top floor. We would go there sometimes for a beer and a look see. It was nick named "The Upper Handling Room" for obvious reasons. That term relates to the area below each turret for handling ammo. Nothing really exciting ever happened to me there.

Well one day Cleve comes up to me and asks me if I would be interested in a blind date. His buddy Kolar has the duty and Cleve's girl friend had a friend and they wanted to double date. I had a girl friend I had met at the academy but she was in New York and I was in California. It wasn't very long before she met someone in New York and that was the end of that. It didn't really bother me. So with nothing better to do I told Cleve that I would be happy to go with him. **My blind date visits the Astoria.**

I think we took the train to the East side of Long Beach to Willow Drive. These young ladies lived with their parents in a mobile home park. Actually these were trailer parks since the mobile homes in those days were true trailers about 30 feet in length. Willow Trailer park was a nice neat and clean park with lots of trees and so forth. So I am led to the Eicher trailer home and knock on the door. These trailers were about 3 feet off the ground so when the screen door is opened, my eyes are about on the level of someone's knees. She had on dark skirt and about all I could see were two rather shapely legs. In spite of what your mother thinks, they still are shapely. I finally looked up and saw a very attractive smiling brunette who answered to Betty.

I really do not remember much about introductions and all that but we went out to a party at some beach home. The party was mostly navy officers and their dates. The thing that impressed me the most about this lovely young lady was that she insisted we walk from the beach house to where we could take a train back to Willow Park. It was a rather long walk and I was willing to call a cab but she insisted on walking. My pay was rather limited about $150/month so that was really neat. This date was in November 1947 and we began to date as often as possible.

We often went to a little bar near the park for beer and dancing. I went with her to her bowling night and bowled as a pacer if someone did not show up. We went to ship parties and such. Her folks would go with us to Knottsberry Farm. In those days it was not so commercial and the food was really great. In February I bought her a bowling ball for Valentine's day and one for me from Sears. I still have mine but one of the kids ruined hers by rolling it on the concrete porch at Hillbrook.

About this time we decided we would get married. I do not remember if I ever really proposed to Mom. We were so compatible that we just knew it was the right thing to do. Things just seemed to follow a natural path to May 8, 1948. Mom had to take some instructions in the Catholic Faith and we were married at Saint Anthony's Catholic Church in Long Beach by Father Clyne. My mother and father were the two witnesses. I do not think my mother was too happy about our whirlwind romance and quick marriage. But she never said anything and I think she finally realized that her son had married a very good woman. I know I did.

I got leave from the ship and we honeymooned at Big Bear lake and Yosemite Park. Jim Hayes let us use his Plymouth car while he and the ship were out at sea. This may have been the time the ship went to Alaska. At Big Bear lake we had a neat little cabin and the people who took care of it were really nice to us. Everything was all set up when we arrived at the cabin near midnight. We had a wonderful time and enjoyed our mountain honeymoon.

When we got back to Long Beach we set up housekeeping in a one room apartment which was merely a kitchenette and living room. The bed was a pull down Murphy bed in the living room wall. 54 years later we put a new Murphy bed in a new house. The woman we rented from predicted that our marriage would last and she was right. The apartment was on a main street where we could get the bus back to the Navy base. Mom worked as a clerk-typist there. Long Beach was the Astoria's home port. While in port I had the duty every third day.

The Astoria was due for a far East deployment in August so we newlyweds were due for 6 to 9 month separation a few months after getting married. Remember that I had missed two short cruises by the marriage leave and taking a pistol team to the matches in San Diego. Both were for about two weeks each. My JO bunkmates were jealous of these leaves so when the orders for our China deployment came out, Hank Clay accosted me with "Let's see you get out of this one." I told him I didn't want to miss the China trip so he didn't have to worry about it. About a month later in the middle of

the night, Hank comes in and shakes me awake with "You SOB you did it!" "Did what?" I sleepily asked. He was in communications and he hands me a Fox sched with a message that Ensign John C. LeDoux was ordered to report to the Superintendent of the Naval Academy for duty as an instructor. Hank never believed I had nothing to do with getting these orders.

The Happy Bride and Groom

CHAPTER XI - RETURN TO USNA - 1948 to 1949

After I reported in we were assigned to housing in a Quonset Village. These Quonsets had two sets of quarters front and rear. They had two bedrooms, a bath, living room and a small kitchen at the rear of the hut. They were also well stocked with cockroaches which about devastated Mom. When we returned after dark, I had to go in first, turn on the lights, and kill as many as I could before she would enter. Of course, air conditioning was an unknown utility in those days and Annapolis is very humid in the Summer. Since it was August we only had a few weeks of hot weather with which to contend.

This short tour was enjoyable in spite of the housing and its assortment of bugs. I only had to work about 15 hours per week as we were expected to enjoy our R&R. Most of the officers on the academy staff were returning from months, even years, at sea. The fifty or so of my classmates who came back to teach didn't really have that excuse but the rules applied to all. This was an experiment to see if young officers could relate better to the midshipmen. I don't know what conclusions were drawn but it was a great tour of duty especially for a pair of newly weds. I got into playing golf since I had the time and the academy had a super course.

I enjoyed the teaching and the various things we could do. Mom and I played bridge frequently with the couple next door LCDR Ford and his wife. They were very friendly and helpful. We also use to go to a little cafeteria in Annapolis that was inexpensive but with good food.

We had one traumatic experience when Mom had a miscarriage. She was about two months along when it happened. She was really upset and I remember trying to comfort her. She just cried and said she would never be able to have any children. Little did she know what the good Lord had in store for her.

While at USNA one of my classmates and I went to talk to the Public Works Officer. This discussion made me think about the Civil Engineer Corps as a career and so I applied for it.

All good things must come to an end and as Spring rolled around we had to expect orders again. We could only stay there for the academic year as we needed two years at sea for promotion to LTjg. So around May my orders came through. Since I had my tour on a combat ship, my new orders were for an auxiliary. I could not believe what the orders said " Ordered to report to the USS Grainger AK184 as Head of the Deck Department." That Head part was the puzzle - I was only an Ensign and most department heads on ships were LCDRs or LTs. Strange, but I soon found out why such things happen. See the next chapter.

My Dad came out to help me drive West as Mom was pregnant with Johnny. She flew from D.C. to San Francisco. Dad and I had an exciting drive through Chicago to California. It was an adventure. We drove normally to Chicago by driving by day and sleeping at a motel at night. When we got to Chicago we decided that with two of us alternating every 4 hours we could get to California in a couple of days. Actually we made it in 36 hours. Along the way we had two flats and somewhere in Nevada we lost all the oil. We were lucky that we were on high ground and could coast almost two miles to a gas station. A bolt had come loose from the oil pan. There was no more adventures and we somehow got to San Leandro to be greeted by our two wives.

The Navy didn't give me much time but ordered me to go to my ship ASAP as they were short of officers. The Grainger was in Hawaii and I was put on a PBY from Alameda. Those buckets are really slow and it took us over 12 hours to fly to Hawaii. We arrived late at night and a jeep was there ready to take me to Ford Island and my new ship. Read "Mr. Roberts" and you know what was in store for Ensign LeDoux. **USNA Bancroft Hall main entrance.**

CHAPTER XII - USS GRAINGER AK184 (1949-1950)

It was about 11 p.m. when I arrived at the pier where the Grainger was moored. The jeep driver took my gear aboard and I was escorted to the Captain's cabin. LCDR Laird was sitting at his desk in his skivvies (it was rather warm). I think he had a glass of whiskey on the desk but he seemed sober enough. He greeted me with a smile and a slightly puzzled look. I think he expected an older looking officer. I think he thought I had just graduated and not someone with shipboard experience.

When he realized that I had some 12 months on a Cruiser he seemed a little relieved. Then he asked me if I was a qualified OOD. "I was on the Astoria, sir" I replied. "That's good enough for me" he rejoined "We leave port tomorrow morning, Mr. LeDoux. I want you to take her out of the harbor" he commanded. With that he bade me good night and the seaman took me to my cabin.

There I was on a ship I knew nothing about in a harbor that I was unfamiliar with and I was supposed to somehow pilot her out to the open sea. I managed to find a petty officer to talk to about the ship and to my chagrin I found out that the Grainger was a single screw vessel. Even the YPs at USNA had a port and starboard engine. The only single screw boat I had ever handled was the 30 ft motor launch we had at the Academy. I was able to find a copy of Knight's Seamanship and review what happens when you back down such a vessel with the rudder to port or starboard. I tried to study the harbor at night and I reviewed the charts and so forth but I was very nervous. I assumed that the Captain would bail me out if I got into trouble.

The next morning I was on the bridge with a crew I did not know. The Astoria had four screws and about 100,000 horsepower. The Grainger had a single diesel engine of about 2500 horsepower with a single screw and later I found out she had a very small rudder.

After morning colors and some introductions to the crew members on the bridge, the Captain said "Take her out". "Aye, Aye sir" I replied trying to not look nervous. So following what I had read the night before, I ordered the stern lines to be let go, put the rudder hard to starboard, and all back on our little engine. When we had moved about 30 degrees from the pier, I ordered the bow lines to be cast off, put the rudder amidships and backed away from the pier. When I thought we were far enough out, I ordered the engine to all ahead one-third. I noticed that it took quite a while before I could sense that we had stopped going back and had started to move forward and turning to the right. On the Astoria you see by looking at the bow line an almost immediate effect in turning. Not so with the Grainger.

I turned to the quartermaster and remarked "She doesn't respond very quickly does she?" He said "No, sir, she doesn't". So with that assurance, I ordered the helm to amidships realizing that she would continue to go right until we got some headway. Somehow we managed to follow the buoys out of Pearl Harbor and into the open sea. Captain Laird had not uttered a word, just a nod of the head. As we cleared land, he went below to his cabin. I had the deck for about an hour and was finally relieved by the next OOD. Later I found out we only had 5 officers on the ship including the Captain and the Exec. That left the 3 of us to do the 24 hours of OOD duty, 8 hours per day, plus whatever other work we had to do in running our divisions.

Now I realized why NavPers had ordered me as "Deck Dept Head". I was the only officer in the Deck Department. Actually I was the 1st Lt, cargo officer, and gunnery officer. Our weapons were two 20mm machine guns, one on each side of the bridge. On most ships the 20mm were the smallest and least effective type of weapon. From time to time, we were able to blow up a few drifting mines.

The next order of business was to get acquainted with my deck crew. The chief petty officer (CPO) was a Chief Cowden and we had 10 other enlisted men. The ship was 238 ft long and about 50 ft wide. The bridge and crew quarters were in the stern of the ship. Forward of the bridge were two cargo hatches and forward of that was the forecastle (fo'c'sle) which rose above the deck well in front of the foremast. Each mast had rigging attached to 2 deck engines used to hoist cargo. They were relatively fast and then we had one powerful engine centered for heavy weights. It moved very slowly. The chief knew how to handle all this gear and the crew seemed ok and worked hard. I found out later some of the crew were on probation from general courts martial. Most of their offenses were for AWOL or desertions. They never were a problem and were able to serve out their probations without further disciplinary action.

If you read the book 'Mr. Roberts' you know that I was the Mr. Roberts of this ship. The villain in the book was the Captain but in our ship it was the Executive Officer (XO). He was a mustang and former Chief Boatswain's mate. Before I arrived, he was the 1st LT and did not appreciate a young academy ensign taking over his old job. Chief Cowden, also a Chief Boatswain's Mate, did not like the XO because he did not think he was a good Bos'n much less a good XO. Also the XO apparently could never remember Cowden's name. So the XO nit picked everything we did around the ship. He would come out on the wing of the boat deck (just below the bridge) and holler some command through a megaphone. We could never understand anything he said, so I would just salute him and yell back "Aye, aye, sir." He was satisfied and went back into his cabin. He never seemed to realize that we never did what he asked because we did not know what he wanted.

Finally, after several months of this harassment, I was able to politely nail him. On a deck inspection of various gear he spotted the end of a line with a grommet weaved in backwards. He began to berate

me and the Chief until I interrupted him with "Sir, that work was done before I got here." Who was responsible? Obviously, this sloppy work was done under his watch, not mine. He looked startled and walked away. He rarely ever gave us any more trouble.

The Grainger was very slow. At full speed with a tail wind we could make about six knots. A person can trot that fast. So it would take weeks for us to get anywhere. We left Pearl for San Francisco. From SF. we went to Seattle; then to Kodiak; then to Adak; back to Seattle; then to San Diego; then to Port Hueneme; then to SF. again. Finally we headed for our home port which was Guam. It took us about 4 weeks from SF to Guam right through Christmas and New Years. The Grainger was logistic support for the Marianas, the Marshalls, and the Gilberts. We brought in supplies and took out Copra, the native harvest of coconut shells that is turned into soap and other products. We often had to pick copra bugs out of our food. There is hardly an island group North of the Equator in the Western Pacific that I have not visited. I was on this ship for about 13 months and we were in our home port about six weeks during that time. So I never thought about bringing Mom out to Guam.

Mom took a train to Seattle to spend a week with me while we were in port. The weather was gorgeous during that week and we had a wonderful visit. She had to stay in a crummy hotel but it worked out OK. She was pregnant with Johnny at the time. **Betty on Grainger in Seattle.**

The officers of the Grainger were an interesting group. The engineering officer was a motor mech mustang who was hated by his crew. When they returned from liberty drunk, they would take an ax from the bulkhead and try to find him. He had to sleep with his door locked and a loaded 45 gun by his side. The communications officer was a former chief yeoman who was afraid of his own shadow. When he was OOD his enlisted watch standers would go to one side of the bridge and claim that they saw a ship's light on the horizon. That would keep him on that side of the bridge the whole watch and they would then goof off on the other side. The skipper usually had a case of whiskey in his cabin. When in port he was never aboard but on shore having a good time. When we were at sea he just stayed in his cabin until we sighted land. He was a very good ship handler and usually piloted the ship into and out of port unless he had me do it. He was really a good guy with some bad habits. So you can see, we had a classic ship with all the personalities you could hope to see.

At one of our island stops (usually in a tropical lagoon) the ship's officers were invited to a party at the officers' club. It was a service white affair and we had to take the ship's boat to the landing. It was the usual type of party with some music and mostly drinking. We were all pretty high when we went back to the ship. To get aboard the ship we had to climb a rope ladder about 15 ft high. As the senior officer, the XO went first. The boat was rocking back and forth and not always next to the ladder. Well the XO was pretty drunk and lost his grip on the ladder and into the water he went. Since he was so popular with everyone, it took us about 30 seconds before someone said "Should we save him?" Of course we did and he never remembered a thing.

Another time we were coming out of an officers' club in our jeep. The road was straight until it came to a breadfruit tree. This tree was about 15 ft wide so the road just made a loop around it. I was sitting in the back sideways to the front seats. A two week reserve officer was in the passenger side and the XO was driving. Again he was a little inebriated and was asking for a cigarette and not watching the road. I happened to look out front and saw this enormous tree trunk in our headlights. All I could get out was "Look---" never got the "out" out. We hit the tree head on at about 20 mph. I was thrown against the front seats and got some bruises; the XO went against the steering wheel and had some severe chest bruises. The poor reservist went through the windshield and cut his neck from ear to ear. As good luck would have it a chief hospital corpsman lived in quarters right by that tree. He was able to save the officer and got him in the local hospital. I think he had like 50 stitches. The front end of the jeep was really a mess. I don't think the XO ever reported this incident to anyone. Somehow we fixed the jeep.

When we went up to Alaska, we fished for salmon in Kodiak and nearly were eaten alive by the biggest mosquitoes I have ever seen. From there we went to Adak to pick up surplus WWII gear left by the Army. Would you believe we loaded up a number of cases of size 12 half soles? Must have really big guys in the Army. Then we had to load cases of foul weather parkas, boots, sleeping bags. They were really neat. The night before we loaded, some of the ship's crew made a midnight requisition. I don't know what all they took but we all had nice warm parkas and sleeping bags. I was the cargo officer and had to sign for everything loaded on the ship. Before I did that I pointed out to the supply officer that many of the cases had been looted and I could not sign for that. He finally gave up and we did not have to sign item by item. I rationalized that a lot of WWII gear like that was just dumped at sea and not taken back to the States.

On many of the formerly held Japanese islands there was still a lot of WWII damage - airplane wrecks, ships still sticking out of the water, bomb craters, damaged coastal cannons and so forth. On Truk I rode a jeep up the mountain to a former Japanese spa. The building had a big bomb crater but a beautiful communal bath was still there. We found out later that there were still Japanese soldiers hiding out in the jungles and they were still sniper danger around. Never saw anything but I was unarmed on the trip up the mountain.

At one of the officers' clubs on some island (Can't remember which one), a former Japanese soldier who was the bartender, took a liking to me and taught me the Japanese stick dance. It's a simulation of two men fighting with two swords but to a fixed routine. You would bang the floor with your sticks and then hit each other's sticks right to left and left to right. Then you increased the tempo until someone makes a mistake. I must have done OK because at the end of each dance he would smile and say "Oh, you number one!"

One last incident about our XO and his skill as a boatswain's mate. On our trip to Alaska we had to deliver a large fuel tank to a Coast Guard station at Scotch Gap. This tank was on the open deck and had to be hoisted over the side and put in the water so the Coast Guard sailors could tow it to shore. Chief Cowden and I decided the best and quickest way to do that would be to wrap some cable around the tank and lift it with the fast winches and just roll it over the side. The seas were rough and we did not want to let the tank bang against the ship's side. But the XO would have none of that. He wanted to use the slow winch and let it down slowly over the side. We told him the sea was too rough but we did it his way. The tank must have hit the ship 15 or 20 times before we got it in the water. I sure felt sorry for those Scotch Gap sailors. They really looked sad and sea worn as they towed the tank to shore.

Captain Laird was really nice to me. He trained me in about every ship maneuver there is: mooring to a buoy; tying up to a pier; going up narrow channels and so forth. He kept saying "Why am I doing this, you are going into the Civil Engineer Corps." It was fun and I really appreciated his patience.

After about eight months, the communications officer departed and I was relieved by another mustang a LTjg Tozco. Strange name. When we got the message of his orders the XO became hyper. He went to the Navy register to check it out. Sure enough it was who he thought it was. The XO apparently really did not like Tozco. It went back before WWII to the Naval Air Station in San Diego. At that time the XO was the station master at arms, the senior petty officer. He must have been doing his usual stellar job because the Commanding Officer brought in Chief Tozco to relieve him before his tour was up. The XO held this grudge against Tozco even though Tozco was not responsible for the change. You could see him wringing his hands in glee since he was the XO, a LCDR, and Tosco was only a LTjg and under his command. I found all this out when Tozco and I became friends. I become Comm officer and Tozco was now 1st LT.

Tozco was part Indian, swarthy and really good looking and in great shape. The XO was fat and rather sloppy. After Tozco came aboard, I don't think Tozco even remembered him. The XO began to really get on Tozco's case. He nit picked everything much more than he did with me. Tozco took it for several days and then demanded a meeting with the Captain. I was there in the chart house with Capt. Laird, the XO and Tozco. Tozco minced no words. He announced to the Captain "If you don't keep this SOB off my back, I will retire to my cabin until we reach port and then I will demand a hearing by a Navy court of inquiry!" The XO was really flustered and the Captain was no dummy. In essence he told him that Tozco was qualified for his duties and to lay off Tozco. That was the end of that!

Tozco and I really hit it off. We both had golf clubs and played whenever we could, Guam and Saipan come to mind. Saipan had a nine hole grass course and you could hire a native caddie, usually young girls, for 25 cents. We paid them more than that but it was fun. Guam had a par three nine hole course with sand greens. Every afternoon that we could play, we had a tropical shower. Tozco's wife came to Guam and she played with us.

Tozco was a character. On Kwajalein we were having a beer at the officers' club during the day. We were about two miles from the pier where the Grainger was moored. It was broad daylight and hot. As we left the club, Tozco didn't want to walk so he said "Let's take this Jeep". Since it was not ours, I mildly objected but got in anyway. As he started the Jeep, some officer ran out of the club to stop us and all he could do was raise the hood and try to disconnect the distributor. He was not successful and we backed away and made a dash for the ship. The hood was still up and how Tozco could see where he was going still baffles me. We made it back and left the Jeep on the pier. The Jeep apparently belonged to the base security officer and we received a mild reprimand by the skipper but that was that.

On one of our island stops we were ordered by General McArthur to survey the depth around a sunken Japanese transport ship. Its stern was sticking out of the water at almost a 90 degree angle. Of course as the junior officer, I had the privilege of doing this. With a few sailors and Chief Cowden we took our small boat to the site and did the soundings around the ship. That was the only time I ever got close to getting seasick. That little boat just rocked and rolled as we did the soundings. Do not know if what we did was OK or even used. I think they were considering refloating that ship.

Another interesting event took place when we were going into Eniwetok, the island that was used for testing nuclear weapons. As the Communications officer I was the only one who knew how to use the decoding machine. Very complicated piece of gear with about 12 wheels of letters and numbers used to decode encrypted messages. Those wheels had to be changed every day from a monthly classified manual. We were waiting for a clearance to go into the lagoon. When the message finally came part of it was garbled right in the place that told us we could or could not enter. Had to request a retransmission. But we finally did go in. When I got the comm job when Tozco came aboard, I had to teach myself how to type since all encoded messages came in a series of 5 letter groups. You can't hunt and peck with that type of message.

Finally the messages came on the Fox schedule. Four times a day routine messages would come via the Fox schedule. On January 24, Two messages, one after another were for me. They were:

JOHN NATHAN LEDOUX BORN 23 JAN 8 LBS 10 OZ STOP
MOTHER AND SON FINE STOP CONGRATS LOVE MOM AND
DAD EICHER

ENS J C LEDOUX USN 498281 WHEN DET BY CO USS GRAINGER
ON/ABOUT APRIL 1950 PROCEED AND REPORT TO PROFESSOR
NAVAL SCIENCE RENSSALAER POLYTECHNIC INSTITUTE TROY
NY FOR DUTY UNDER INSTRUCTION IN CIVIL ENGINEERING.
REPORT NO LATER THAN 15 MAY. EXCESS TRAVEL TIME TO
COUNT AS ANNUAL LEAVE. PRIORITY AIR TRAVEL AUTHORIZED.

I did not get off the ship until April when we next were in Guam. Flew from Guam on a Navy cargo plane to Midway and Johnson Island and finally to Pearl Harbor. Commercial flight from there to Los Angeles. Mom was jumping for joy as I was and I finally saw John, my 3 month old son. He was very sober and was looking over Grandma Eicher's shoulder and wondering who that person was who was kissing his mother. It was a red letter day.

Numero   One   Johnny

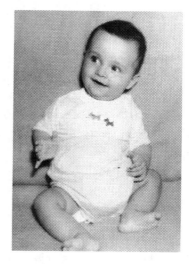

CHAPTER XIII - RPI YEARS - 1950/51

This was one of the few times that we traveled across country that we did not drive. The Navy flew us to Schenectady, New York. We were met by an old shipmate from the Astoria, Bill Spangler, who had transferred to the Civil Engineer Corps while still on the Astoria. In fact he was the one that made me curious about the CEC. When I relieved him once on an inport watch, his uniform no longer had a star above his ensign's stripe but something that looked liked crossed bananas. Actually they were crossed oak leafs. I asked him what the insignia was and he told what little he knew about the Corps. That's why I checked out the Public Works officer at the Academy when I was there. I liked what he told me and so I applied for transfer. It was the last year I could do that. I was thinking about submarines or flying before that. Joe took over the submarine bit almost 40 years later. In my day you had to have two years of shipboard sea duty before you could apply for anything else. I was faced with seven years of sea duty so the shore type duty with the CEC (SeaBees) looked very good for a newly married man with a son. Remember that I was slated for the CEC when I was at Cal and going to Case Institute if I did not make the Academy. Small world.

At this time Rensselaer (RPI) was the only university that the Navy was using to convert line officers to the CEC. I was still a line officer recently promoted to LTjg and it turned out I was the senior line officer in this group at RPI. The 30 officers became known as the "LeDoux Group". A retired Admiral Combs was the Professor of Naval Science at RPI so I reported to him. As group leader I had some additional duties besides study but they were minimal. One of the officers in this group was Donn Ashley from an earlier academy class and he was a full LT but already transferred to the CEC. Since line officers take precedence over staff officers I was IT. There were several classmates from 48A and 48B and the rest from 49 and 50..

We had a good group except for one lazy character that would do little work and expect us to help him. He was not dumb just lazy. When he failed several courses in the first semester, I told Admiral Combs to send him back to the fleet because he was a poor officer and would be trouble wherever he went. Old Lady Combs was too kind hearted and would not do it. The end of the story is that he never made LT but was passed over twice and was booted out then. I felt sorry for his wife who was a really nice girl. She did not deserve a jerk like that. How he graduated from USNA is a mystery.

RPI was a very tough school. We had to take all the civil engineering courses in 3 semesters plus two summer surveys. We had 21 to 24 units per semester. Since they were all engineering courses and mostly math based, I had little trouble. In fact I think I got straight A's. Based on that, I was invited into three honor fraternities CHI EPSILON, TAU BETA PI, and SIGMA XI. The first was the civil engineering frat, the second was like Phi Beta Kappa, and the third was for research. It was an honor but not something that I worked for.

We had a number of golfers with the group. Donn was the best. He had about a 5 handicap. He helped us all. We tried to play at the municipal course in Schenectady every Saturday morning. It was a great course and we had a lot of fun. Donn knew all the tricks. Once Donn and I were playing two guys who had never played the course before. We were playing a par three and they had the honor. Donn takes me aside and tells me to take out a 3 wood and practice swinging it. "Donn " I said "It's only 160 yards!" I usually use a 5 iron. He told me the hole was deceiving and he was trying to game them. Well they looked at us with fairway woods and looked puzzled. They knew Donn was a long hitter so they just shrugged their shoulders and took out their fairway woods too. They both hit way over the green and we went back to our irons and hit on the green. We both laughed our heads off and they had to laugh too. They had been had!

The housing provided was built for WWII GI Bill students and they were bare bones and ramshackle. But we were all in the same boat except for Donn. He had money and rented a nice apartment in town. The housing was on a hill above the campus about a 10 minute walk. All our classes were in the same engineering building. There was virtually no free time during the day and we all had to work very hard to get it all done. All except our lazy friend that is. We walked in the heat of summer and the snows in winter. Even though it was hard work, I really enjoyed all the courses with the exception of soil mechanics. That seemed too theoretical to me.

Our group was very athletic and we managed to win most of the intramural sports we entered: touch football, softball, basketball. We were nicknamed "The Old Men" since we were about 5 years older than the typical student. RPI at that time consisted mostly of men students. I remember that once in awhile we would see a woman engineering student. Even then there was some debate whether or not that person was really a woman, if you catch my drift. Sometimes a comment would follow like "I wonder where she wrestles tonight". We never were distracted by cheerleader types.

Cal Perkins, a 48A classmate, and I decided to save money by buying a side of beef and cutting it up in family size packages. There was a freezer plant in town and we bought the side there. I told the butcher that I would do all the cutting since I knew how to do it and we knew how much to put in each package. He agreed but I think he thought we would make a mess of it. So when the side came in, we went down to the butcher/freezer plant and went to work. I did the butchering and Cal and the girls did the wrapping. The owner of the shop was impressed with my skill and asked how I came by it. When I told him I was a journeyman meat cutter before I went into the Navy. He asked me if I would like a part time job with him. We worked out a schedule and the money really helped. My only stipulation was that I would not wait on customers. He had a lot of farmers who brought their hogs in so I had to do a lot of ham and bacon preparation with brine pumping and so forth. He was a nice young man to work for and the arrangement was mutually beneficial. How I had time to do that and do the homework required at RPI, I have no idea. We sure ate good from then on. It is interesting to note that this was the only time in almost 25 years in the military that I had to do any "butchering". Never had to fire a shot at any enemy.

We had a **survey each summer.** The first was a route survey or laying out a highway route. The second was surveying a small town in Vermont. We worked in small groups and had to do all the surveying and drawing required. Both were for several weeks and we had to live away from RPI. After the day's work we played golf. Twilight lingered to almost 10 up there in

56

Vermont. After golf we played bridge until midnight. We managed about 6 hours of sleep per night. We played with the same partners in bridge and the cumulative scores were astronomical. Bob Miller and I played against Donn and his partner. One hand was hilarious. Bob and I had a great night making a number of slams. On this particular hand, I won the bid with a 7 spade, a grand slam. After the dummy was laid out and the first card was played, I looked at the board and remarked "Donn, if you have the queen of spades, this is a lay down". Donn was on my right. He just took his cards and threw them over his right shoulder in complete disgust. That ended that night's play. Donn is on the right in the picture on last page. I am on the left.

On the second survey, we were in Vermont and Betty was back in Troy. She was pregnant with Duffy and due any time. Remember I was in the Pacific when Johnny was born and as luck would have it I was gone again when Duffy arrived. I got the telephone call and had to rush back to Troy. By the time I got there, Betty had just delivered Duffy. That was the good news. The bad news was that the Doctor told us that he was born with bilateral club feet - both feet were turned at 90 degrees and the soles were facing each other. We should have requested an orthopedic specialist to treat him but we didn't know any better. The doctor did the best he knew how by putting casts on Duffy's feet. We were due to leave shortly for duty on the West Coast at Point Mugu Missile Base so we thought it would be OK. The doctor did not advise any differently. By the time we got him to California and had the orthopedic surgeons look at him at the Oak Knoll Naval Hospital in Oakland, he had been in the initial casts for almost a month. The Navy doctors were quite upset and said he would need a lot of treatment for at least two years. They informed NavPers of the situation and I was transferred from Mugu to the Naval Air Station at Alameda so he could get the treatment he needed. Duffy's feet needed three types of rotation for complete correction and the top orthopedic surgeon at Oak Knoll said all three could have been done at birth and the whole process would have been completed in months instead of the four years it took.

Jeff (Duffy) about two

CHAPTER XIV - ALAMEDA NAVAL AIR STATION (1950-1953)

Alameda was one of the few stations where we had quarters. We were assigned a little 2 bedroom house just outside the main gate. The street was dead ended so it was a nice safe place for the kids to play. It was also near one of the runways so there was some noise at times.

Alameda was a major overhaul and repair station for Navy aircraft. I was assigned to the Public Works Department and was given the job of Overhaul and Repair liaison. I had to supervise the O&R work that Public Works performed. The department and the station itself was under the command of line officers, like I used to be. This had impact on some of the events that happened. **LeDoux's at Alameda..**

One of the first things I noticed was that the civilian workers in the O&R department were doing things that were Public Works responsibility. They had various blue collar trades and when O&R work was slow they did some things to the buildings without going through the normal process. Many times they did not do a very good job and often violated safety concerns. I brought this to the attention of my boss, CDR Curren. I was amazed to find out that Curren was deathly afraid of line officers as if they could do no wrong. He did not want to rock the boat. I brought my concerns to the CAPT and XO of the O&R department and they assured me they would correct things. They never did. This went on for several months and I was really getting frustrated and angry.

Well thank God for Murphy's Law! One Monday morning as I drove into the station, I noticed a strange pattern on one of the O&R hangers. There was a bright rectangular pattern where the paint was fresher than the surrounding surface. I could not remember seeing this before. So I began to investigate. Finally on another building I found the answer.

Over the weekend the O&R workers had moved a structure from the hanger and put it up on another building. This was a 10 ft I-beam that had a hoist attached to one end used for lifting small weights from the ground to a second floor area. The I-beam was welded to a plate that had been attached to the hanger wall. The new arrangement looked strange to me and I found they had welded two pieces to the plate to make a U shaped device that was hung over the parapet wall of the new building. Why did they not anchor it to the wall? I broke out the plans for this building and found that the parapet wall was just a cinder block false front. The hoist was able to lift about 2000 lbs. With great glee I knew I had these SOBs where I wanted them.

The workers that moved the hoist had no idea what a moment was. This is a force acting along a moment arm tending to cause rotation. With 2000 lbs of weight and a 10 ft arm, there was 20,000 ft lbs of turning moment. Cinder block could not resist such a force. If they had tried to use the hoist, the whole device would come crashing down on whoever used the hoist. Could easily have killed someone. Knowing that my boss did not want to rock the boat, I decided to call the brass to the site. I called the XO of the station, the CAPT of O&R, the station safety officer and my boss to meet me at this building. They all asked what it was and I just said you have to see this. Imagine a lowly LTjg asking all the brass of the station to go somewhere at a moments notice.

Well to their credit they all came within 15 minutes. I told them what had happened over the weekend and what the safety facts were. The safety officer was aghast. The O&R Captain turned red. The XO was livid. I then mentioned a few other safety things that O&R had done and asked the XO to make the O&R people stop doing what Public Works was supposed to do. My boss just stood there smiling. The XO complimented me for being observant. He really gave the O&R boss a severe dressing down and told him that he never wanted to see something like this happen again. The O&R CAPT was really mad at me and told me that I should have come to him first. I reminded him that I had done just that a number of times with no action by him. He just turned around and left. For someone who had ordered a LCDR off the bridge of a ship this was duck soup. I loved it. After all, that O&R Captain did not write my fitness reports.

My boss must have caved in to O&R for the very next week I was transferred to the AROICC (Assistant Resident Officer in Construction Contracts). That's where I wanted to be anyway. New construction is more fun than maintenance. The AROICC was a LCDR who played golf so we got along fine. We had a number of large and small construction projects going on - extending the runways out into the bay for jets; new O&R building; new supply warehouses and some other minor work. My office was now away from the main PW office in a shed like building. I had 20 inspectors working for me headed by an old Irishman, Dan Hanify. I was able to bring my secretary from the PW office, Jean Ford. She was a really great secretary. Dan was OK though he talked too much and I thought a little too friendly with some of the contractors.

When Jean and I arrived for our first day, the outgoing officer gave us a brief tour and overview of the projects. He assured me that Hanify had everything under control. This was all new to me but the first thing I found out was our files were a mess. Everything was just filed in chronological order. Some things you only see once and never really need again. Change orders and progress reports were different. So Jean and I decided the first order of business was to reorganize the contract files. The change orders needed a separate file. So did progress reports so partial payments could be made. This took two weeks but this reorganization allowed me to be in the field every day and not just be doing paper work at the office. We organized out going correspondence by various categories since many were quite repetitive. All I had to do was put a little note on each incoming letter with a notation of what reply category was needed. Jean took care of the rest. This took me only 30 minutes a day and I was free to see what was going on. Hanify seemed a little put out because the last guy seldom left the office. "Hey, Dan" I assured him "All I want to do is learn".

Well I am a quick learner and soon Dan realized I was no pushover. I found concrete too sloppy and ordered more field slump tests. The contractor's estimate of completed work did not line up with visual observations. I made them turn in more documented progress reports and held up payments until their payroll reports were available. The contractor's attitude began to change and they became more alert to their obligations.

When I first arrived the contractor building the runways was submitting a massive change order because more fill was sinking in the bay than originally estimated. He had a just claim for more money but I knew he was going to ask for more than was really justified. I insisted on getting every truck load record on amount of fill and distance carried. There were hundreds of them and I had to record and check all of them. We had no computers then and this was all hand work. I really was trying to be fair but his estimate and mine were off by a factor of two. I was confident of my work and told him what the Navy would allow. He refused our offer and said he would go to court. We told him to go ahead. In court my meticulous records won and his sloppy estimates lost. He was paid based on my work which was really fair. After it was all over he even complimented me on what I had done and said when I left the Navy to let him know.

One other problem was interesting and the solution was even written up in the Civil Engineering Journal. The new O&R building was a square building 500 ft on each side. It was a reinforced concrete slab with column footings every 50 feet. The floor was designed for 250 lbs/sq ft. The subcontractor who was erecting the interior steel columns and beams bid on the basis of using a motorized crane on the floor because of the large distances from the outside. When he was ready to erect the frames we found that the vehicle he was planning to use and the weight of the steel frames and girders would exceed the 250 lbs/sq ft design limit of the floor. He was told he could not use the crane he had in mind. The A&E would not give a waiver since he had no idea what the true limit was. There was a safety factor but he would not take the risk. The poor contractor said he would go broke using a more primitive method. He was told to propose something else. Well he did. He proposed to put two new axles and eight more wheels on the vehicle. This would drop the expected load to well under the 250 lbs/sq ft. We gave our OK with the stipulation that these new wheels had to bear the weight and not just be dummy wheels.

Alameda was a true learning experience in many ways. Jean's husband was a bus driver but also a scratch golfer. He really helped my game by only working on one correction each round.

Janelle, our first girl, was born at Oak Knoll Naval Hospital and now our brood numbered three. After these two years, orders came through sending me to the Norfolk Naval Supply Center. **By this time I was a full LT.**

CHAPTER XV - NORFOLK AND CHEATHAM ANNEX (1953-1955)

When I received orders to the Supply Center in Norfolk, I assumed this was just a routine assignment. Before I could report to Norfolk I received verbal instructions to stop at the Bureau of Supplies and Accounts (BUSANDA) in Washington D.C. There I was met by a CDR from the Civil Engineer Corps and a Supply Corps Captain. Apparently my reputation at Alameda, especially the hoist safety problem, caught the attention of BUSANDA and the CEC. They told me that I would be the first engineer at the Supply Center in 20 years. They suspected that technical things were not under control at the Supply Center and they needed someone on the inside to find out what was going on. "You want me to be a spy?" I asked in jest. "Something like that" they replied in unison.

So off we went to Norfolk. We had driven cross country this time in a relatively new 51 Buick I had found in San Diego. We found a house in Little Creek that had a large back yard. Nice place for kids. It was about 5 miles from the Naval Base.

When I reported in to the Supply Center I found that I was on the Commanding Officer's staff. He was a Rear Admiral and he seemed like a nice guy. I reported to a Supply Corps Captain. When I asked him what my duties were, he said he did not know since I was the first engineer they ever had. "Just do your thing" he told me. I was given a desk and a phone on the sixth floor in a big room with no dividers. Everyone around me was a civilian clerk of some type.

My first day was a classic. I don't think the Admiral or the Captain I reported to were in on the spy thing, since my orders were to send information directly to Washington. About 9 a.m. as I sorted out a few pencils and a few note pads, an electrician came by to change some fluorescent lights above my desk. He put up his step ladder and removed two bulbs and then left. I assumed he would return shortly since he left the ladder and other gear.

During this time I studied the Organizational Manual for the Center and found that one of the big departments at the Center was the Labor Department. This included many technical shops like the Electrical Shop, the Carpenter Shop, the section that loaded ships and box cars and so forth. This Department was headed by a Joe Crosswhite, a high level civilian, who had been in this job for close to thirty years.

The electrician did not return by noon when I went to lunch. I made a mental note to see what the workload of the electrical shop was since at least one man had so little to do that it took all day to change two fluorescent tubes, a five minute job. I decided to visit Crosswhite's office to get a tour of his empire. He was a big, heavy set man, who struck me as the politician type. He had come up through the labor gang which now had about 1000 people in it. He was nice and condescending to this young officer and assigned the tour to his second in command. This gentleman was about 35 and appeared to be cooperative. At least he talked and I listened.

The tour lasted about 2 hours and the major impression I had during this tour was that every shop I visited had a number of men who were just sitting around, drinking coffee, and shooting the breeze. I asked what sort of system they had for assigning work and checking on completion. There was no system. Each shop seemed to run their own little empire with virtually no checks and balances. I did not make waves but made mental notes for future investigation. I did find out that aside from shop skills this organization had no engineering skills. Crosswhite assured me that the Public Works Center on the Naval Base was available if they found any problems. Most problems do not tap you on the shoulder and scream for attention. You have to be able to recognize a problem in the first place.

Early in the first few weeks, I went up to Cheatham Annex, a back up supply depot about 50 miles North. There was a LT, CEC, there who showed me around. It was a really nice base with quarters, a swimming pool, piers to fish off, woods and peace and quiet. I resolved to relieve LT Acuff when he left but said nothing.

As I began to investigate the true workload of the Center, I estimated that there was at least a 30 percent over staffing at the center. Some of the shops were doing work that the Public Works Center should be doing. Almost a duplicate of what happened at Alameda. Working with Washington we began to develop a plan to establish a public works department staffed with CEC officers and civilian engineers. This ultimately happened and Joe Crosswhite's empire came tumbling down. After the PW Dept was set up, the labor force was reduced by some 300 people over a period of one year. LCDR Foster Lalor was the first PW officer at the Supply Center. But this did not happen overnight, it took almost a year to accomplish this feat. To get it in motion we needed some sort of bombshell to get all parties to agree to it. Well, Murphy's Law again came to the rescue.

THE FUEL LINE OVERHAUL DISASTER

A few months after I had arrived and we had started working on the PW Dept establishment, I made a tour of the various out buildings and piers. One of the piers had a nearly completed major project of replacing the 16 inch fuel lines that serviced fleet ships. I thought it would be interesting to look at it.

On the pier I met the PW Center inspector. He must have been close to 65 and looked like that old character on Saturday Night Live. There was nothing to see on the pier surface. All the work was under the pier. I asked this old gentleman when he had last gone under the pier for an inspection. He said he was not able to do that because of his poor physical condition. He merely accepted the contractor's reports. "Do you mind if I take a look?" I inquired. He, of course, had no objection.

I did not check with the contractor but went to my car for an old pair of overalls that just happened to be there. Went down to the waterfront and finally found a punt (squared ended row boat) and paddled myself out to and under the pier.

The view was shocking! The pipe line expansion valves were hanging loose and about to break. There were many rusty parts of the pipe where hangers had cut through the insulation. It looked like the renovation should just be beginning and not ready to accept. Gleefully I realized that we had the ammunition for the need for a PW Dept The PW Center should have found these problems. A local PW Dept would certainly have been on this project on a daily basis.

Back in the office I called BUSANDA, BUDOCKS, the PW Center and informed them that we had a major disaster with this fuel line project and they better get down to Norfolk PDQ. It was just like Alameda only many times bigger. Within the week all the Brass was there confirming my findings. Even the Architect & Engineer firm had to be there. It turned out that the A&E had made an error in calculating the thrust when the quick closing valves closed. Fuel oil in a 16 inch line has tremendous inertia while fueling a ship. The valves to the ship are closed in less than a second and the fuel then runs to the U turn at the end of the pier. The structure there was not strong enough to resist this force and that's why the expansion valves tore loose from the pier. The fix required about $300 thousand change order and the A&E had to admit their error.

That put the icing on the cake relative to the need for a PW Dept. With a PW Dept my job at the Center was finished. LT Acuff was resigning from the Navy and the PW Officer's job at Cheatham was now available. So I got the job that I really wanted

.CHEATHAM ANNEX

We moved into temporary quarters for about a month until Acuff left and then we had the PW Officer's quarters. There were 4 duplexes at the far end of the station on the James River. The grove had many tall trees and behind the quarters was a sloping hill down to a playground for the kids. The officers' pool was only a short distance from the quarters. The quarters were well furnished and had ample space for a family with three kids. It was the best situation that we ever had in the Navy. There was a good security fence around the yard so it was safe for the kids. They just loved that little hill and the playground equipment at the bottom. The station gardener had an area where he grew vegetables. Trees with very tasty apples were also available. Cheatham Annex was an old Dupont Powder factory and had about 3000 acres of forest. The station buildings occupied only 250 of those acres. With the game available and fishing off the two piers, you could almost live off the land. The station also had two fresh water lakes with boats available for fresh water fishing.

Sounds ideal doesn't? It was for Betty and the kids. I had to work long hours and seldom had the chance to really enjoy it but I was able to do some fishing off the piers and participate in the annual deer hunt. Every evening you could drive through the warehouse area and see 20 to 30 deer running about. Once we saw a big buck in an area not far from the house.

The PW Dept at Cheatham had about 250 employees most of whom were skilled at various trades. We even had a railroad with two groups for it: maintenance and operations. There was a cold storage plant, a cargo pier and a fuel pier. Back in the woods there was a sizable fuel depot with many fuel tanks. Near the main gate we also had a back up diesel plant in case we lost power. So we had considerable responsibility for power, roads, building maintenance and construction. There was also a fleet of vehicles and an auto repair shop. We had an apartment complex for some of the civilian workers. While I was there we built a new bowling alley for recreation. In an old barn like building, we had a movie theater. In effect it was a small rural village.

As you know, I always looked a lot younger than I actually was. Once when I was almost 35, in Levis and a tee shirt, I was carded when I was buying some liquor for my Dad. A full Navy LT with 10 years of commissioned service! As you may remember the skipper of the Grainger had the same first impression. The head civilian honcho at Cheatham was a PW foreman, Bill Phillips. Some time later our secretary told me that when Bill first saw me he told her that he would wrap this young LT around his little finger. Bill must have been about 50 at this time. We eventually became good friends. He was in for a shock when he quickly found out I had a mind of my own.

One of the driving passions in my life has been to work hard - a day's work for a day's pay and then some. I have little patience with slackers and gold bricks. In every government organization I have been associated with, I did my best to see that the tax payers got their money's worth. There is always slack in every outfit government or civilian - you just have to root it out. Before I got there, Cheatham Annex had a reputation for being a recreational spa for Washington brass. It was so lush that CNO had a slot in the pier for his barge. Drew Pearson, the predecessor to Jack Anderson, wrote a column slamming the Annex for illegal endeavors like sending barrels of oysters to various congressmen. Most of his charges were ill founded but there was some truth to it. I was determined to stop such things during my watch.

LT Acuff must have been a desk sitter. That is not my style. I like to see what is going on and you can't do that from a desk. Two things I learned when taking over a new job. First follow the paperwork and secondly manage your time. The first thing I did at Cheatham was to take every report we had to produce and take it personally to the next addressee with these questions: what do you do with this? Do you really need it? Most of the time it was not used and therefore could be eliminated from our workload. One of the ways I managed my time was not to take any phone calls before 11 a.m. except from the Commanding Officer. These two things allowed me to get in the field where my men were working to see that work was necessary and efficiently done. I don't think Bill Phillips appreciated me sticking my nose in his business. That was too bad. Another thing I learned was to listen to the ideas or complaints of the workers especially the lowest guy on the totem pole. You can see more looking up the chain than the top guy can who usually gazes at the horizon. A few illustrations support this concept..

One day as I drove around in my pickup truck, I found 4 carpenters sitting on their duffs by the road. They were supposed to be building a bus stop shelter. "What's the delay?" I asked . "We're waiting for the surveyor to give us an elevation" they replied. I got out of the truck, asked for a stake and a hammer, hammered in the stake so it was about road level, and said "There is your elevation, now let's get going!" They did not know that I was an expert at driving in stakes from my Utah days.

Another time as I drove by the Cold Storage Plant, I saw 6 men gathered around part of the loading dock area. I went over to find out what they were doing. They were preparing an area for a concrete pour, a space about 10 by 15 ft. I looked at two of the older guys and asked them if they could do this job. They said they could so I sent the other 4 back to the shop for another assignment. I was beginning to suspect that here too, we were over staffed.

Not long after that I walked by the carpenter shop about 2 p.m. and through the window I could see 10 or 15 men just standing around. I went to my office and waited 30 minutes then asked Bill Phillips to go to the carpenter shop and see how many men were there. He came back and said there were 15 men getting their assignments. It was now 3p.m. I suspected that these guys were through for the day and just waiting for quitting time. "Bill", I said "I was by there 30 minutes ago and those same 15 guys were standing around. How long does it take to assign jobs and get them out of there? We still have 2 hours left". He looked startled because he did not realize I had been there that long ago.

After work that night, I sat down with Bill and instructed him that starting next week I wanted each shop to lay out their workload for the next 2 to 4 weeks. Each job had to be estimated for time and materials and then at the end a comparison between estimate and actuality. I told him I thought we were over staffed and if we were, we would begin to cut back through attrition, not a RIFs (reduction in force). That was the beginning of a new day and before I left we had reduced the PW dept by almost 50 jobs. Some of the men even admitted to me that they were glad because they did not enjoy goofing off.

One day I found an electrician changing a light bulb in a street light. We had a string of these along the main road and some of the side streets. How long does it take to change one light like that I asked him. "About two hours with travel to and from the shop" he told me. They only changed a light when it went out. "How long would it take you to change all the street light on the station" I asked. About 3 days he said. I told Phillips to have all the street lights changed and not do it again until 20% had gone out. Then all would be changed again. Lights are cheap but labor is not. I also found out we were having electricians change lights in the quarters and apartments. I had all quarters and apartments stocked with an mix of lights and told the occupants to change their own lights.

People are funny. Apparently the railroad operations and maintenance leaders had been having a feud for a long time. I asked Bill why he let this thing go on. He said he didn't know how to stop it and they usually got their work done. I told Bill to bring them both into the office. They came in and sat sullenly without looking at each other. I said something like this "Bill tells me you both know your own jobs and I believe him. But I will not put up with this feud any longer. It is damaging to your men. I don't care what the feud is about but you two settle it or within one month one of you will be gone from Cheatham. I don't know which one yet. Now shake hands, makeup, and get out of here." They sheepishly shook hands and I heard no more about their feud. I don't know how I would have fired either one but the threat worked.

Remember the surveyor? Apparently he was a communist sympathizer and he constantly was causing trouble. I told Bill we were going to get rid of him. "How?" Bill asked "He has veteran's preference". "Can he do any other job?" I asked. "I don't think so" he admitted. So I just reorganized the department and eliminated the position of surveyor. He appealed and things hit the fan. It took 6 months with all kinds of hearings but we convinced all that we only needed a surveyor occasionally and could get one from Norfolk. His elimination stood up. He was gone and so was a lot or our personnel problems.

Finally a human interest story. As I mentioned before I had to get out and visit various parts of the base. In my first month I made a point of talking to everyone in the PW dept. Way out in the boonies was the incinerator run by an old black man. I went out there and talked to him for about 20 minutes to see if he had any problems or suggestions. He had none. Before I could leave, he said respectfully

"Sir, you is the first boss man I ever did see!" "Thank you" I responded "Keep up the good work and we will see you again before long." He had a big smile on his face.

Since I was the only boss man on the base at night, Bill Phillips taught me how to start the diesel generator in case we lost power. One stormy night, the kids were watching TV and the Davy Crockett series. Lightning struck and we lost power. The kids just looked at me and cried out "Fix it Dad". I jumped in my pickup and raced to the power house. Kicked in the diesel and we had power again. The off base power was out for several hours before we could stop the diesel. It was fun doing that and the kids thought their old man was worth something at last.

In 1954 Cheatham was directly in the path of hurricane Hazel. The eye actually passed right through the base. It did not hit full fury until late afternoon but it was blowing pretty good when I went home for lunch. There I found dear Mom and the kids in the yard looking at the rough water on the river. I rushed them back into the house amazed that they were outside. After the storm there were some big tree limbs on the ground right where they had been standing. A large tree in the back just missed our house. We had a lot of damage to the warehouses with walls caved in and most of the roofing gone. It took weeks to clean up and repair the damage.

Mother nature is something else when she loses her temper. A large cargo ship had come up from Norfolk and tied to our pier assuming they would be safer at Cheatham. At the height of the storm, the wind was blowing directly against the ship toward the other side of the river. The ship was tripled up with 2 inch lines around the pier bollards. Next morning the ship was aground on the other side of the river. Each bollard had eight one inch bolts into the pier concrete foundations. The force of the storm had sheered off all these steel bolts and flung the bollards across the ship into the river. Those who saw this happen claimed it was like a sling shot going across the ship. Other evidence of the storm damage makes you appreciate the forces of nature and what wind can do.

We were at Cheatham for only one year. Jimmy was born January 15, 1955 at the army hospital at Fort Eustice. I had applied for Post Graduate school and was the first CEC officer to receive nuclear training. We were ordered to report to Monterey for PG training in nuclear physics. So we had to leave in June. By that time we had finally managed to buy a new car - a 1955 Chevrolet station wagon. I look back at Cheatham Annex as one of my most challenging assignments and one of the most rewarding. I think the PW guys were sorry to see me go, even Bill Phillips.

CHAPTER XVI - PG SCHOOL/MONTEREY AND OAK RIDGE

We again had quarters at Monterey - Wherry Housing or something like that. Quite small. We had to squeeze the four kids into one bedroom with stacked bunk beds. Otherwise the one year there was very enjoyable. Mom never did like the morning fogs but the scenery there was spectacular with 17 Mile Drive and the ocean views. Managed to play golf at Pebble Peach for $20. It now costs about $300. Just the walk and all those gorgeous houses along some of the fairways was worth it. I vividly remember the 7th hole, a very short 105 yd par 3. The high wind was directly behind us. I hit a low 7 iron punch shot that was near perfect. The ball landed in the middle of the green bounced up and the wind blew it into the ocean. My next attempt stayed on and I one putted for a bogey. I shot an 87 which was good for that course.

Post graduate work this time was harder than at RPI. Advanced physics, chemistry and math courses. Some of the math courses covered areas I had never heard of like Legendre Polynomials. Never really found the opportunity to use any of it. They had to devise a special curricula just for me. My degree was in Nuclear Physics but I had more exposure to nuclear reactors for power plants.

Nothing very humorous or strange happened in Monterey. While there 10 of us took group golf lessons at the Navy driving range. The pro there was an authentic Scotch pro named Burns. Really nice guy and the lessons only cost $1 for each lesson. He was a good teacher and did not try to make Sam Sneads out of us. He just tried to maximize whatever potential we had. He only worked on one thing for me for every lesson. He said I was looping at the top which was essentially a baseball hangover. My right shoulder was coming around horizontal instead of underneath causing a pull or a slice. He brought me from a low ninety shooter to a high seventy low eighty shooter, about how I still play. I broke 80 for the first time at the Del Monte course with a 78. Thank you Mr. Burns.

After one year at Monterey, we had to go to Oak Ridge, Tennessee for the final touches in reactor engineering. The school there was the only one in the U.S. that taught reactor engineering. It was ORSORT (Oak Ridge School of Reactor Technology). While in Monterey we bought a camping popup trailer to save money on the trip East. The trailer was about 8 ft long and made of aluminum. The top half folded out and rested on the ground. A canvass tent was then erected over the whole thing. Quite ingenuous and easy to pull. The trip East was an adventure that Mom would like to forget. In the mountains I had to unhitch the trailer, turn it around by hand, move the car and rehitch. All on a narrow road. We were able to get most of our money out of it by selling it in Oak Ridge about a week after we arrived.

ORSORT was one of the best schools that I ever attended. The class had about 120 students in it mostly from industry. We had about 20 Navy officers mostly from the Rickover program. The class was divided into small 4 to 5 man groups and assigned to group study rooms. Our group had a civil (me), mechanical, electrical and industrial engineers. We had three lectures in the morning and afternoons were devoted to labs or problem solving sessions. The problems assigned were real life type problems that sometimes required a few weeks to solve. The labs were at the Oak Ridge reactors and again this was real life exposure. For graduation we had to write a thesis usually in groups of 2. My partner was a Naval aviator who also came from Monterey. He was also a good golfer and we played together frequently at the Oak Ridge Country Club which was free to the students. Our thesis was the hazards associated with a sodium cooled reactor. It must have been OK since we both graduated.

We all were housed in apartment complexes in Oak Ridge. Very small and crowded but we survived. The only funny story happened when Mel (an office room mate) and I were bowling one afternoon. Another student dropped by who had never bowled and asked how the game was played. So I gave him my usual overview and demonstrated the art of aiming at the marks and not the pins. I told him that I bowled a curve and that if I could make my ball pass over the second mark from the right, the ball would hit in the 1-2 pocket and usually a strike would result. Well, wouldn't you know it, I bowled 8 strikes in a row and had a 277 game. The visitor thanked me and remarked that the game looked very easy. Mel and I just had a good laugh about that. Years later I ran into Mel when he was at the AEC. We both brought up this crazy incident. **Judy age 3 to right.**

Oak Ridge was memorable for a non academic reason: Judy was born there. Our little Tennessee lass. This time the birthing took place in a civilian hospital.

Next Chapter news article and a Nevada A-Bomb crater about 300 feet across

68

CHAPTER XVII - PORT HUENEME, NCEL AND CECOS

After finishing at Oak Ridge, I had orders back to the West Coast to NCEL (Navy Civil Engineering Laboratory). The brood now numbered five. With a small baby we decided that Mom would take the girls, Janelle and Judy, and fly to California while I would take the boys and drive West. My brother Richard came out to help me with the kids. The station wagon had a foam pad in the back so the kids could sleep when they felt like it. We made a few memorable stops along the way: Lookout Mountain in Tennessee and Carlsbad Caverns in New Mexico. I drove in 12 to 15 hour stretches and then rested for a full day at a few places. Richard watched the kids while I slept and rested. We only took 4 days to get to California. Mom was staying with her Aunt Lenore in Pasadena.

We had temporary quarters in a base Quonset hut until we found a 4 bedroom house to rent on 5th Street in Port Hueneme. Hueneme was an old Indian name meaning "resting place". When I was on the Grainger, we stopped once at Port Hueneme and I thought it looked like the end of the world. From the land side view, it turned out to be pretty nice place. While there I was promoted to LCDR

My first skipper at the Lab was CAPT Art Chilton. He was like a second father to me since he was the one responsible for setting up the nuclear PG program for the CEC. He frequently visited me while I was at Oak Ridge so it was great to be with him again. A Nuclear Division was established with me as Director. Sounds rather grand but I only had one other person in the Division, a LTjg Albright. NCEL was involved in the nuclear weapons testing program both in Nevada and the Pacific. Our job was to design structures to withstand the blast, thermal and radiation effects of nuclear weapons. My job was to analyze the radiation penetration of structures. We found that 3 ft of earth cover was sufficient to eliminate most of the initial radiation so the main problem was the radiation remaining in the fallout after the initial blast was over.

After Chilton left he was relieved by CAPT Merdinger. Chuck Merdinger was an interesting guy. He was a survivor of Pearl Harbor on the battleship USS Nevada. After the war he was an Oxford Scholar studying bridges through history. He also introduced Lacrosse to the Brits since that was his sport at the Academy. He was an accomplished and entertaining after dinner speaker. One of the things he required of all lab researchers was to get papers or articles published. I didn't like the idea at first since writing was not my long suit. But after I began to get articles published and getting money for them, I changed my mind. The culmination of all this writing, some 30 or so articles in various publications, was the Toulmin Medal for the best article in the Society Of Military Engineer's journal for 1960. I had to go to Washington D.C. to receive the medal at the SAME annual banquet. I was told that this was the first time that this award had received an unanimous vote. The article was "Nuclear Power: Promise and Problems".

The lab was an interesting place to work as they had all kinds of stuff going on there. We had a good golf group and I bowled on the lab team in a local league. Once again I rolled a 277 to take the high scratch game for the year. CAPT Merdinger, though an athlete himself, did not go along with the Navy tradition of "Rope Yarn Sunday". This was essentially a Wednesday afternoon time to get all the various rope work repaired and brought up to date. In other words sort of a free afternoon. So those who were not into rope weaving and such could take the afternoon off to participate in sports like golf. Under Merdinger you could not do that but he was all in favor of participation in Navy base sports. So I just ended up as Captain of the Pistol Team, was on the base golf and bowling teams. I was gone a lot more than merely Wednesday afternoons but the good skipper thought that was great. Mom did not like it since I had to make trips to San Diego and Las Vegas with the teams. I just did that to spite the Captain and his resistance to Navy tradition.

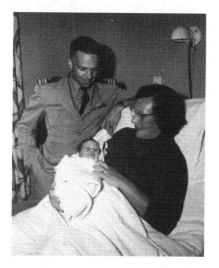

In 1960 Jean was born. She arrived closest to the SeaBee anniversary and so became the 1960 **SeaBee Baby of the year.** We got all kinds of gifts for that event. That year I was also transferred to the Civil Engineer Corps Officers' School (CECOS) at Hueneme as the Executive Officer and Academic Dean. **Betty and baby to right.**

CECOS (1960-1962)

The mission of this school was to train newly commissioned officers on how the Corps ran its business. There were three areas that had to be covered: new construction, SeaBee duty; and shore maintenance. These classes lasted six weeks and we had 6 or 7 classes per year. The school also had a number of short 2 week courses for senior officers and civilians. I taught the radiation aspects of our Protective Construction series that taught the basics of protection from nuclear weapons. By this time I was a **LCDR. See picture below.**

The commanding officer of CECOS was a CAPT Mark Jordan. He was a very strict CO but on the

whole not a bad guy to work for. To illustrate how nit-picky he was, one morning when I came in he called me into his office. You could see he was just short of blowing a fuse. "Did you see where the staff car was parked?" he demanded. I replied that it was parked in its usual place. "Go look again" he nearly screamed. I did so and reported that it looked OK to me. "It's not centered in the space!" he bellowed. Sure enough, the rear bumper was just over the back white lines. So I had the enlisted driver park the car exactly in the center and then painted a white strip just below the driver's window so he could always park it properly. The Captain seemed pleased.

Another morning he complained that the

window shades were not all at the same level. So forever after we had the duty enlisted man make sure all shades were the same before the skipper came to work. Aside from those two incidents, we got along just fine.

One of the first things that Jordan and I changed with BuPers was the rank of the officer instructors. We had four civilian instructors and 12 officers. Many of the instructors were ensigns and lieutenants junior grade. High ranking officers and civilians often attended the school and it did not seem right to have such low ranking instructors. So we managed to change the policy with a requirement that every instructor had to have 2 things: a master's degree in the subject taught, and 10 years of experience. After that was in effect we had full LTs and LCDRs as our instructors. So they knew their subject areas. They only had to learn how to teach. A major step in that direction was sending each new instructor to San Diego to take the enlisted teacher's course. This was a two week course that taught how to lecture, use movies, blackboards, felt boards and so forth. We then took turns to sit in on lectures to help improve each instructor. One of the most effective methods of helping was using a movie camera to record a lecture and then letting the instructor see his own performance.

The main classroom was redesigned by eliminating windows that caused distractions when pretty girls walked by. A color scheme was installed that made students focus to the front of the room. The instructor had a console at the lectern where he could control the movie and slide projectors, the screens and the classroom lights. It was a great room for teaching. CECOS was one of the finest schools in the country. This was demonstrated during the Cuban Missile Crisis. Because of the potential nuclear threat with Russia and the general lack of engineering expertise about this threat in the civilian engineering community, the Department of Defense asked CECOS to put on a series of short courses for civilian engineers. We used the two week Protective Construction courses and started within a few weeks to train engineers from all the major A&E firms. CECOS put on 10 of these courses consecutively right through the Christmas holidays. There was about 40 students per class. It proved to be a huge success and put CECOS on the national map.

A number of civilian engineers came with reluctance because they didn't think they could learn anything from military engineers. They found that these two week courses were tough and crammed with information.. In order to get all the information across, the course started along three different tracks that came together on Friday. This caused some confusion and concern the first few days of each course. Every Wednesday night I went to the school. The students would be there reading, studying and doing problems every night until near midnight. My purpose was to assure them that if they hung in there these first few days, that by Friday they would see how it all fit together. By the end of the two weeks they realized they had been through a unique learning experience. We received many letters from these men after they returned home extolling the course, the instructors and the fact that the taxpayers were really getting their money's worth at CECOS.

An engineer from Seattle talked to me the last day and told me how his attitude changed even the first day. He said when he received instructions that he was going to a Navy school his first thought, as an ex-marine, what a waste of time to be lectured by a bunch of shave-tails (i.e. ensigns or LTjg's). He came under protest. The first hour he began to change. I would introduce the staff and briefly tell them what they would learn. Then Bud Vance, also a LCDR and structures expert would start them off. "Well" thought this Seattle engineer " at least they are not shave-tails." By the end of the 2nd hour he was beginning to hit the panic button. "How can I learn all this stuff in two weeks?" The respect begins to grow and he thinks "Hey these guys are pretty good." By noon he thought we were all geniuses and he would never catch up. After graduation he told me that this was the best learning experience of his life and that CECOS was a super school. We later received a SecNav award for this.

Because of my "expertise" I was invited to speak before a number of organizations. The message was one of hope since with adequate preparation a society could survive a nuclear attack. This was received with some skepticism by the press until I convinced one reporter to sit through our course and then to take a course in Washington D.C. prepared for journalists. He became a believer and a supporter of mine.

During this time I had a running newspaper debate with none other than Linus Pauling the famous Cal Tech chemist. I found out that he was a communist sympathizer and he was trying to discredit me. He was writing false information. I finally nailed him with one of his scientific journal articles that was published a few years before this. In my last letter, I said let us hear from a famous scientist and quoted directly from his journal article that refuted his newspaper letters. My last sentence was something like this "Who is this famous scientist, why none other than Dr. Pauling himself. Dr Pauling, which of your two views do you now stand up for?" He never sent in another letter.

Because the threat of nuclear war was in the forefront of most people and in the press, I was asked many times to speak before civic groups. My basic theme was always that we could survive a nuclear war if we prepared for it . At that time the Russians had fallout shelters for most of her people. All we did was talk about it. My coverage in the newspapers was what started my debate with Dr. Pauling. I was invited to be the keynote speaker at the University of New Mexico at a conference of university engineers. The speech was received very well. Recently, I found a copy of the speech and my first aside in the speech brought the house down. It went like this: "A red alert sounded and this man and

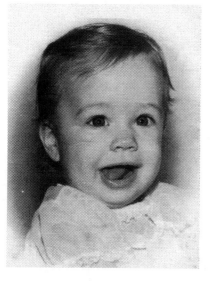

his wife ran to their fallout shelter. In a few minutes, they heard a loud banging on the door. The man asked 'who is it?' The reply "Marylin Monroe". The man later described what happened. ' I can still hear her screaming as I shoved my wife out the door.' "

The two years at CECOS were now up and orders were expected. The Office of Civil Defense asked the Navy to assign me to them for a period of time. So once again we were headed cross country now with six kids. This was going to be our last cross country trip in the Navy although we did not know it at this time. We had moved coast to coast eight time in nine years.

This is the 1960 SeaBee adorable baby of the year.

CHAPTER XVIII - - KANSAS STATE AND CIVIL DEFENSE

Before we moved to the nation's capitol, Civil Defense asked me to participate in their summer institute at Kansas State University. KSU was located in Manhattan, Kansas so I took a train and left Betty and the kids for this six week adventure.

Art Chilton, now retired from the Navy and a full professor at the University of Illinois, met me at the station and took me to a house that he and Dr. Lew Spencer had rented for the summer. These were two brainy guys, way above my limited physics background, but they treated me like an equal and we had a great time living together. The meals we fixed were an adventure each night but somehow we lived through it all. **Lew, Jack and Art at left**.

Art's job was to run the field experiments. Lew taught the physics background and I taught the applied engineering. The students were an international lot, from England, Germany and the Far East. The Office of Civil Defense was spreading the word as far as possible that survival in the nuclear age was a distinct possibility. It was a lot of hard work but there was time to socialize and enjoy a hot Kansas summer. Bill Kimmel, Head of the Engineering Department, and his wife Kathy were great hosts and we had dinner with them at least once a week. Kathy was a true Kansas farm girl and she could really cook. The corn on the cob was the best I have ever had. Manhattan also had a nice 18 hole golf course that I somehow found time to play. One of Bill's staff had a very nice swimming pool that we used almost every day after classes were done.

Based on my experience at CECOS where we had a foreign officer's course every year, I wrote to the Kansas City Royals and asked for free tickets to a baseball game. They came through with over 40 tickets and everybody had a great time, especially the non-Americans. I tried to explain the game to the group before the game started and wouldn't you know it, the first batter hit the first pitch out of the park for a home run. The foreigners thought that this was a common occurrence. They learned that it was not, as the game progressed.

After the six week institute was over, I took the train back to California. We packed up and again drove across the country to the Washington D.C. area. This time we had six kids in our station wagon. We drove through the desert at night right through a sand storm. In the Arizona mountains, the engine just stopped. We were miles from anywhere and it was dark. I thought we would have to stay right there until morning. Within 15 minutes a car stopped behind us and the driver asked if we needed help. The Lord was with us that night, because that driver was an auto mechanic. He quickly found a broken distributor wire which he fixed by twisting two wires together. He told me to get it

73

fixed as soon as possible. The car started right up and we were on our way. Got it fixed at our first stop that next day.

The routine each day was to get up early, about 5 a.m. pile into the car and drive until about 8 or 9. The kids slept until we stopped for breakfast. We drove until 3 or 4 p.m. and stopped at a motel with a pool. While the kids used the pool, I tried to rest a little before dinner. We stopped in Columbus, Ohio so Mom could show us where she had lived and where she went to school. At that Columbus stop, we almost lost Judy. I was resting in the motel room and so was Mom. The kids were using the pool. Judy could not swim and somehow had jumped into the deep end. Duffy, Janelle and Johnny were alert enough to see Judy was in trouble and somehow the three of them pulled her out. Really scared us!

Before I went to KSU, I had made a trip to D.C. to talk to the Civil Defense people about working for them. The Navy said it was OK but I could still turn it down. I had vowed not to go to D.C. until I made Commander because it was too expensive. While on this trip, I was able to find a nice house in Annandale a few blocks from Annandale High School. Very nice neighborhood. The house was essentially one story with three bedrooms but it had a full basement that opened up at ground level in the backyard. It had been vacant for a year and never lived in and the price was down to $22,500. So when we arrived in the area we had a house. The moving van arrived shortly after we did and we moved in to our new house in Annandale in 1962.

THE PENTAGON

The Office of Civil Defense was located in the Pentagon. I was assigned to the Secretary of Defense staff and reassigned to Civil Defense. I found 4 other military officers in our neighborhood to car pool to the Pentagon which helped on the car situation. The group I worked with was an engineering and education office headed by Jim Roemke. He had been at KSU on several visits and it was his office that set up the institute. I guess he liked what he saw in what I was doing and so asked the Navy for me. Jim was a great person and he organized a staff of 4 other engineers, all civilians. The goal of this office was to educate the engineering profession on how to evaluate and design structures that could provide protection from the effects of nuclear weapons.

Our first objective was to educate engineering professors in summer institutes like the one at Kansas State. These professors in turn, would train engineers and architects with 16 week night courses in various metropolitan areas. I lectured at six summer institutes and also taught these 16 week night courses. One of these courses was in Pennsylvania and we flew there in a small charter plane. Janelle and Duffy went with me on one of these flights.

During this two year period we trained about 10,000 engineers in these principles. My major contribution to all of this was the development of simplified engineering charts and tables that made building analysis easier, quicker and cheaper. The basic physics documents generated by the National Bureau of Standards (Lew Spencer) were very obtuse to the practicing engineer. I was able to reduce these basic physics books (about 3 inches thick) to a little booklet about 5 pages long. My colleagues at Civil Defense called me the champion curve plotter of all time. Most of this work was done while I was at CECOS and then Civil Defense included this method in the text books that we used. The Navy awarded me the SecNav Achievement medal for this work.

While at Civil Defense I was on a National Academy of Science sub-committee dealing with nuclear weapons and their effects. I was also a member of the White House Engineering Advisory Board. One of our tasks on that board was to develop methods of protection for the President in the event of a nuclear attack. We made several visits to the White House war room. Had a glimpse of Jackie Kennedy on one of these visits. We also spent a week at Camp David working on our various ideas - some of which were really off the wall, like our proposal for a rocket ready to launch from the White House grounds. Most of our work consisted of hardening shelters in the White House and at Camp David. The Camp David week was really neat. Cozy cabins, Ike's putting green, and great food. Marine security there was like something from a James Bond movie. Working at the Pentagon was also interesting. You could really get lost in that place.

Even though I left Civil Defense in 1964 to head up the Navy Shore Based nuclear power program, the Director of the Office of Civil Defense nominated me for the Captain Robert Dexter Conrad award for scientific achievement in November of 1966. His letter can be found in the appendix. Nothing ever developed on this award but Mr. Durkee's letter was appreciated.

Whenever you see one of those civil defense signs on a building indicating it as a fallout shelter you can take some pride in the fact that your forebear John C. LeDoux played a key role in evaluating that building.

The family tribe was rounded out with the birth of **Joyce in '63 and Joe in '64.** They were born in the Army hospital at Fort Belvoir. So we now had eight children. It was a good thing there were no more moves in sight. At one point we were thinking of putting together a family cartoon titled "Eight is too Many".

The work I did for the Civil Defense program at CECOS and in the Pentagon was recognized by the award of the Achievement medal after I transferred back to Navy headquarters as Director of the Nuclear Division.

ACHIEVEMENT MEDAL

CHAPTER XIX - SHORE BASED NUCLEAR POWER

This chapter could be called "The Poor Man's Rickover". Admiral Rickover was instrumental in developing the Navy's nuclear powered fleet. He started by developing the first nuclear powered submarine. He was a very unique man and accomplished his goals against very great odds. I had incidental contact with him but never met him. One of my ASTORIA shipmates, Bill Bass, was one of his key assistants. I once visited Bill at his home and the poor guy hardly had any peace even at home. I really felt sorry for anyone who had to work for Rickover in spite of his obvious accomplishments. There is a book on Rickover called "Blow Negative" that is fiction but apparently quite accurate on his character.

By this time **I was promoted to CDR.** Before I reported to the Naval Facilities Engineering Command (NAVFAC), I requested a trip to the Antarctic to get familiar with the PM3A, our nuclear power plant at McMurdo Station. As the Director of the Navy's Shore Based nuclear program, I felt it was essential to go there. This has to be one of the most interesting trips I have ever made. We flew from Andrews Air Force Base to San Francisco, then to Pearl Harbor, and finally to New Zealand. I can not remember the total flight hours involved but it was a long flight, close to 12,000 miles.

NEW ZEALAND AND THE ANTARCTIC

The Deep Freeze main base was in Christchurch, New Zealand. We were outfitted there with our Arctic cold weather gear and had to wait for a flight to the ice. One of the members of our group was a Captain Jim Whiteaker, a member of CNO's staff. He was also a golfer and naturally we became close friends. He later played a major role related to my job at NAVFAC. We ended up spending about 10 days in Christchurch before we had a flight to McMurdo. Well, wouldn't you know it, about a half mile from Deep Freeze headquarters, was a private golf course that was open to Deep Freeze personnel at no cost. Jim and I played there every day we could and had a ball. We were the only players on the course. Even the members were not in view. It was quite a beautiful course and somewhat challenging. The only thing I remember was that I made a career putt of close to 110 feet. Paced it off.

Occasionally we made a trip into Christchurch to see how the New Zealanders lived and played. They were very friendly and we had fun talking to them. New Zealand is essentially a rural country with high mountains and primitive roads. Once I went to a local restaurant expecting to order some native Maori chow. The menu prominently showed they served "Maryland Fried Chicken." I was able to order some native soup but otherwise it was a disappointment. Because it was a rural nation quite distant from where hard goods were made, such things as cars, refrigerators and so forth were very expensive, about 4 times what you paid in the states. As a consequence, the people took very good care of these things with a view to making them last a lifetime. I rode in a Stanley Steamer, for example, that must have dated back to the early 1900s. The social life in Christchurch revolved around one of the local hotels. Everybody gathered in their main room for drinks and talks. For those who like to hunt and fish, New Zealand is the place to go.

Well we finally made the flight to the ice in a C135, Navy Cargo plane. There were no seats, you just found a place to sit on the floor. We were in our Arctic gear with parkas and air boots. The boots had a jacket surrounding your feet that was insulated by air. We also had those long heavy gloves that came up to your elbows. We had to leave all our normal clothing back in New Zealand. I had my 8mm camera with me and took a number of reels during the trip and on the ice. You may have seen it. The flight had a point of no return. Once you arrived at that point the plane had to continue to McMurdo and could not turn back to New Zealand in case of trouble. I took some shots out the window at that point and you could see the ice flows on the ocean. If the plane went down after that no return point, even if it made a good landing, survival was measured only in minutes.

Since you are reading this story, we obviously made it to McMurdo. Upon landing we were transported in vehicles that could travel in the snow. At McMurdo, we were housed in the McMurdo Hilton, a quonset like building. As we flew toward the ice, the sun rose on the horizon. It would never set during the summer at McMurdo but was about 15 degrees above the horizon 24 hours per day. This caused some to suffer an ailment called the "Big Eye". With the sun up 24 hours a day, you became somewhat disoriented not knowing whether it was day or night. Your whole sleep cycle was messed up and it was difficult to go to sleep with full daylight outside. Without proper sleep, your eyes stayed open and actually looked big, so you had the "Big Eye" syndrome. I must have caught the "Big Eye" since I double exposed part of the movie film.

The mess hall was open continually and you eat whenever you got hungry. For those working outside, the average daily intake was close to 6000 calories. As a result, if you were part of the wintering over crew you actually developed a layer of fat below the skin as protection from the cold weather. It never got above freezing at McMurdo, though the summer weather was quite pleasant, about 20 degrees above zero. You could walk around in shirtsleeves because the humidity was so low. One of the hardships at McMurdo was the latrines. There was no indoor plumbing. You had to use a facility that exposed your derriere to the crispy outside air. One did not read something while doing your sanitary business. In and out as quick as possible. Also you did not take any showers since it was healthier to not do so.

Except for several visits to the PM3A power plant, we had time to sight see the area like a tourist. The New Zealand base camp was a short walk. It was interesting because they had a large number of Husky sled dogs. The Ross Sea was next to McMurdo and was still frozen over. You could see and sometimes hear the packice as it collided with shore based ice and would rise 15 or 20 feet high in places. Once I explored a tunnel in the packice that led down to the sea floor. It was about 2 feet wide in places. I only stayed there about 15 minutes but took some movies of it. We also visited Scott's hut that was on a arm of land that stuck out into the Ross Sea. That hut was built about 1906 when Scott was making his trip to the South Pole. The food inside the hut was still perfectly preserved since the temperature was always below freezing. Scott's group got within a few miles of this base on their return from the pole. But a blizzard hit and they all froze within sight of their base camp. Very sad story. You could almost still feel their presence in that hut since it looked like they had only just left it. There was another monument there to some sailors that lost their lives.

THE SOUTH POLE

One of the purposes of my trip was to explore the feasibility of putting a compact reactor at the South Pole. One of the problems in the Antarctic was fuel for power and heating. The PM3A, though only a 2500 KW plant, conserved enough fuel at McMurdo to make the refueling of the South Pole station earlier than before the PM3A was built. At that time, there were several companies that claimed they could design a nuclear power reactor that would almost fit into a 55 gallon oil drum. Such a plant would almost eliminate the need for fuel oil at the pole.

After about week Jim and I were able to get a flight to the Byrd Station and the South Pole. We flew in a C135 that had cargo for both bases. At Byrd we had enough time to walk through the base. This base was constructed by digging huge ditches about 40 feet below the surrounding terrain. Arctic huts were placed in these trenches and then compacted snow arches covered the trenches. That ice was as hard and as strong as concrete. The sides of the trenches had ice crystals that looked like diamonds. The temperatures in the trenches outside the huts was always about 50 below zero. This base and its structures were very stable compared to what we found at the South Pole.

I was able to sit on the flight deck on the trip to the pole. The view was spectacular. We flew roughly over the area that Scott had to travel on foot. You had to admire the courage of explorers like Scott. Flying was a piece of cake. That is, until we arrived at the South Pole . The C135 was equipped with ski landing gear. The South Pole area in about 10,000 feet above sea level and is flat as far as the eye can see. The landing area was outlined by 55 gallon oil drums but was not much help. The pilot could not tell how high he was since the instrumentation was not that accurate. All you could see was miles and miles of white. As I listened on my ear phones, the new pilot gave me great confidence as he made his approach with this remark "My God, this is really hairy!"

Somehow he landed the plane. The tail gate was opened and we all had to hurry out. The cargo was essentially jettisoned on the ground, outgoing passengers were rushed into the plane, the tailgate closed and the plane took off. The plane could only stay on the ground for 5 to 10 minutes and had to leave before the hydraulics froze. As the plane struggles to take off in the freezing very light air, you had to wonder if you would ever get out of this place.

The South Pole base was a Rube Goldberg dream. Initially it was an above ground structure but over time, the heat within the building melted the ice on which it stood, and it slowly sank. The day we arrived, it was a nice summer day at 65 degrees below zero. We walked down into the main building and found that the floors slanted in many directions. There were numerous gutter like drains hanging from the ceiling that drained water leaking from the ceiling into buckets and barrels. There were places where a reactor plant could be located but that would have to wait until the construction of a new base building.

While there I walked out to the place where a barber pole stuck out of the ground. This was supposed to be within a hundred yards of true South so I guess I can say I stood at the South Pole. We ate in the mess hall and shot the bull with the crew. I understand that there is about 7000 feet of ice over the land mass. The ice cover grows very slowly. The Antarctic is classified as a desert since there is relatively small new moisture. The usual weather circles the Antarctic and moves old snow around the continent. Bare ground is exposed over many places. The crew told me that in the middle of Winter, the temperature can drop to 150 degrees below zero. That allows a man only minutes outside to read some instruments. At least one person committed suicide by just walking away from the base building during the Winter. As luck would have it we were able to fly out the next day and returned to McMurdo.

Antarctica was an interesting place teeming with life in the sea and the many penguins on the shore. Birds were also plentiful. Our mission completed, we then had to wait for a flight back to New Zealand. Then we had to wait for a flight back to the states. We had a week before that happened so we played more golf and went on a picnic along the coast with some of our New Zealand friends. I have always wanted to go back to New Zealand to see more of it. It had a climate about like Northern California. The scenery is truly outstanding.

While awaiting our flight back to the states, I received orders to go to Australia. Apparently some defense official heard that a nuclear weapons expert was in New Zealand and asked for my services while down under. That part of the trip was paid for by the Commonwealth of Australia. So instead of going home, I headed West to Melbourne.

AUSTRALIA VISIT

The Australian civil defense people met me in Melbourne and took me to my hotel. I found out that this trip had been arranged between our Office of Civil Defense and theirs. The purpose of my trip was to run a short course for Australian engineers on the design of fallout shelters per our American method. From Melbourne I was flown to Canberra their Capital and gave the one week course there to about 20 engineers. I had a limousine available for my use and had some free time to look over Canberra and their War Memorial.

Met a reporter there and we became friends. He invited me home for dinner one night. It was amusing how he had to explain to his kids how Americans used their knife and fork differently than the Australians. I told them that their method was better and more efficient than ours. The course was successful and I enjoyed my visit. Managed to play golf there too. Took a trip to Sydney and then back to Melbourne for my trip home. The flight home was via an Air France plane that stopped at Tahiti but could not get off the plane. After reading "Mutiny on the Bounty" I had always wanted to visit Tahiti. At least I was there once even though I never saw one of those Tahitian hulas.

THE POOR MAN'S RICKOVER JOB (1964-1967)

The position at NAVFAC was due to be my last Navy duty. It was a real challenge. The Division had 5 civil service engineers and 5 officers at Fort Belvoir, a group at Port Hueneme, and the crew at McMurdo. I found that the officer I relieved had relied almost entirely on the officers and the civilians were not utilized much. I changed that on day one since these GS13s and GS14s should have much to contribute. This decision paid off with high morale and loyalty to me.

We had a force of almost 120 officers and men with only one job - running the plant at McMurdo. The next 2 crews were at Fort Belvoir undergoing extensive training on a duplicate reactor at this army post. The reactor crews were a mix of Army, Navy and Air Force personnel since the Department of Defense had vague plans for more shore based nuclear plants.

This was a large number of personnel to run one small nuclear plant. Training took about 18 months so we had one crew on the ice and two crews in training. The training was rigorous and similar to the Navy submarine training. We were able to select the cream of the crop from Navy SeaBee enlisted men. They were an outstanding group. One of the first things I did was to warn everyone that the program was in danger of cancellation because of the number of people in the program doing only the one thing - operating the PM3A at McMurdo. I had a feeling that Admiral Corradi, our new boss, would be taking a critical look at the program. We had to expand our program before we were cut off. So we began to brainstorm how to expand our responsibilities.

One of our strengths in personnel was in health physics. There were a number of health physics offices scattered throughout the Navy. None of them had the quality of personnel that we had. So I went to see Jim Whiteaker at Navy HQ to sound out the idea of concentrating all Navy health physics offices under our centralized control. He agreed that would be a good idea but it would be tricky to do. He suggested that we would have a conference in Washington of reps from all the Navy commands to discuss centralizing this function. Each command was to propose how they would handle it if this function was centralized in their command.

While this was going on, we thought that we ought to get the Navy into the radioisotope generator business. A number of companies were getting into this area and were building small generators. We talked to these companies and got their attention since use by the Navy would help them expand into the civil market. These experimental generators were costing millions of dollars in research funds but my office only had about $350,000 per year of funds I could use. Several companies like GE and Martin agreed to sell us generators at nominal cost like $25,000 just to get them used somewhere.

About three months after reporting to NAVFAC, Admiral Corradi asked me to brief him on our program. We put together a program of Navy Health Physics, isotope generators, and shore based nuclear power. One of our power proposals was a 20 MW reactor for Guam. Guam had three fossil fueled plants with a weakness that fuel oil had to be shipped in. If such fuel could not be shipped into Guam, the whole island economy would be in jeopardy. Guam was an important defense island and the proposal made a lot of sense. With a power plant on Guam we could make use of our crews by rotating them from a cold climate to a hot climate and maximize all their training. None of these things had been approved. They were all just ideas. Admiral Corradi liked what he saw and gave us his blessing.

Now we went to work in earnest... We got the health physics job and put that organization together with training and administration. We decided to market the generators by putting out a catalogue brochure describing the generators that industry had available at that time. We sent the catalogue to all Navy commands for information.

THE FAIRWAY ROCK PROJECT

Within a month of distributing the catalogue, I received a call from the Electronics Lab in San Diego. They needed one of these generators for a project in Alaska. Most of these generators put out very little power, like 25 watts, but they could be put anywhere since they were independent of the atmosphere. Deep sea, mountain tops, even the moon were possible locations. There is a small island between Alaska and Russia that the Navy used to monitor submarine traffic, ours and theirs. It actually was a rock, not an island - Fairway Rock to be exact. The top of this rock was 600 feet above the ocean and about 3 football fields in length. The Navy was using a propane generator to provide power to several sensors in the ocean. The propane generator could only be operated about 7 months of the year because winter weather would snuff it out. They only needed a few watts of power for the sensors so our isotope generators were exactly what they needed. The call came in August and I asked "When do you need it?". "Yesterday" they replied. "It will cost you about $25,000 just for the generator" I told them. "Money is no problem, can you get one for us?" they asked. I told them I would get back to them as soon as I could.

I called Martin in Baltimore since I knew they had a 25 watt generator sitting on their dock. This was fueled by Strontium 90 a radioisotope obtained from waste fuel from nuclear power plants. It was a gamma emitter with a 37 year half life. The heat produced the D.C. power from thermoelectrics. This little generator was contained in a leaded container that weighed about 6000 lbs, about 3 feet long, and 2 feet in diameter. I asked Martin if they would release it with payment sometime in the future. They were enthusiastic at the prospect.

Now we had a generator but how do you transport a 6000 lb object from Maryland to an offshore rock in the Bering Straits? We contacted the Air Force since they were flying supplies to Viet Nam on a daily basis. The Air Force said they had a plane leaving Dover Air Force Base in 10 days that could handle that object if we could get authorization. Through Jim Whiteaker's help I went to CNO's office and an Admiral Anderson (surface at the pole fame) signed an authorization message to the Air Force. The Army had an outfit at Fort Dietrich that was authorized to move radioactive material. They agreed to take it to Dover. We got the AEC to authorized a license to move the object within the United States. This took about 4 working days. The final problem was getting it to the rock from Alaska. A ship would not do because of the 600 foot elevation. A big chopper had to be found.

We contacted the Navy in San Diego and all their helicopters were busy. They told me that a civilian bush pilot in Alaska had a chopper that could handle this load. So I called this guy and he sounded like an Alaskan bush pilot. He at last agreed to do it but we had to position some fuel along the way because of the distance he had to go. We managed to get the Army Corps of Engineers in Alaska to take on this task. Finally we had the Coast Guard provide a ship to follow the chopper to Fairway Rock in case the generator dropped into the sea. It all went without a hitch. Within 10 days of that call from San Diego the generator was on Fairway Rock. One of my guys went there with a rep from Martin to hook up to the sensors. Most of this was done with phone calls and letters with no financial papers at all. It took six months to get everyone paid. We had the cooperation of several branches of the Army, Air Force, the Coast Guard, the AEC and one gruffy bush pilot to accomplish what appeared to be impossible. I still can hardly believe we did all this with no red tape or bureaucratic interference. To close out the story, about 15 years later I visited my old office and asked about the Fairway Rock project. "It's still running and we have never had to service it" was the amazing reply. Martin had agreed to refuel it if necessary after 17 years but I do not think they ever did.

We put a generator in the Marianas trench, 35,000 feet down. We helped with the plutonium generator that was put on the moon. There was a number of applications that followed the Fairway rock project. Based on this expertise I made several trips to London and Vienna, Austria, for international meetings on the use of these generators. I think oil companies use them as markers for oil wells in the ocean. The 20MW reactor concept for Guam got to the President's desk but was not approved.

In 1967 I was in the zone for Captain but this would have obligated me for 4 or 5 more years. With kids approaching college age, I decided to retire and go into the civilian market. I was 43 years old and to this point had a remarkable and interesting career. My civilian staff petitioned the Secretary of the Navy to create a GS15 civilian job for me to stay as director. I thought this was really a vote of confidence since several of them were GS14s and eligible for such a job. I thought about it, but decided I should go outside of the Navy and see what it was like. So in June of 1967, I was retired from the Navy and went looking for work in the civilian world.

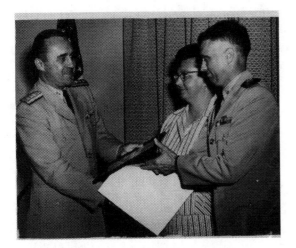

RETIREMENT CEREMONY

One of the things that influenced me to retire was a remark that little Joe made when I returned from one of my many trips. Every time I left on a trip Joyce and Joe would wave and call out "Bye-Bye" as I drove off in our decrepit Renault. About this time, Joe was about 3, as I entered the house returning from a trip, he greeted me with a smile and a hug and said "Hi, Bye!". Obviously, I was gone too many times. **So I retired in 1967.**

CHAPTER XX - POST NAVY LIFE (1967-2003)

Thirty five years have passed since I retired from the Navy. My civilian career was interesting but not nearly as much fun as Navy life had been.

My first job on retirement was Director of Flow Corporation's Nuclear Division located at Fort Belvoir. Flow was a Boston company that had a contract with Civil Defense to run some field radiation studies. This was an attempt to simulate the effects of fallout from a nuclear weapon. We used a Cobalt 60 source that circulated in a plastic hose laid out in a pattern on the ground. Co60 emits high energy gamma rays similar to what fission products would produce. This job lasted 3 years until Flow was bought out and our contract was terminated.

I then became a consultant to another Boston company to represent them in Washington. We had some interesting ideas to market. One of these was an artificial heart powered by plutonium that worked like a coffee percolator. We worked with one of Dr. DeBakey's assistants but were unable to sell the idea. I also did some consulting on the side to make ends meet.

After this I was hired by Bob Weiner in Baltimore as Vice President of Marketing. Again using contacts in Washington to generate contracts. Two contracts were interesting. We won a managerial contract to run the clean car project. The idea was to produce ideas for cleaner running cars. The ideas were tested in Ann Arbor, Michigan. All kinds of cars were proposed from electric cars, to fuel cells, to cleaner running gas powered or alcohol powered vehicles.

We won another contract with Johnson and Johnson to develop a small refrigerator for dentists using epoxy for fillings. Two chemicals are mixed together to produce the filling. The dentist only had a minute to mix the two chemicals before placing the mix in the filling. These chemicals had to be kept at a low temperature near the patient's chair. Using thermoelectrics we designed a unit that was the size of a shoe box that could be placed on the arm of the chair. Our design won the contract. Mr. Weiner got greedy and decided to bid on the manufacture of these units. Against my advice and several others in the company, he set up an assembly line to make the units. With little or no manufacturing experience, our low bid won but it bankrupted the company. Another job search began.

BOULDER 1973-1976

Based again on my Civil Defense work, I was offered a job at the University of Colorado to run a professional advisory office funded by Civil Defense. This Boulder office was responsible for 5 Western states: Utah, Colorado, Nebraska, North and South Dakota. We would contact the owners of prospective new buildings and their A&Es and show them how to incorporate protection from tornadoes and earthquakes with little increase in cost. It was called "slanting". The real purpose was to provide protection from nuclear weapons.

This job did not require a full 40 hours per week so I was able to work on my MBA. Almost made it but still need about 12 more credit hours. It was fun and I was usually the oldest student in the class. During one of the marketing classes, students had to make a presentation about some marketing principle. Our group won the prize for our presentation when we demonstrated how to get a client's attention. We hired a belly dancer to introduce our presentation. She certainly got the attention of the class and the professor as she jangled her way across the class platform. The Prof. gave us an "A" for our project.

In a class on decision making, each student had to interview a local business and determine what techniques we learned in class could be applied to that business. With many years of experience in the real world, I knew that most decisions were a one shot deal and were based on the best information available at the time. Once a decision is made subsequent actions usually reinforce that decision. I thought the theories in the course were a little unrealistic so I asked myself "What business must make repetitive similar decisions on a near daily basis?" Like a flash it came to me. Professional football!!. So I wrote a short note to Mr. Ralston the coach of the Denver Broncos and asked if I could see some records of their games. Within a few days he sent me an invite to visit their headquarters. He welcomed me, introduced me to a few of the players (most of them are so big I felt like a dwarf). He showed me the file room and where the game records are kept. "If we have two copies, you can keep one. Otherwise you can copy whatever you want." I acquired about 10 years or game records. Each record covers 3 or 4 pages and each play is recorded in meticulous detail. In short I used this information to write a linear program to determine the strategy that would maximize yardage on offense and minimize yardage on defense. It was interesting because the program said that first and ten plays were a passing down and not a running down, contrary to what pro football preached. Since almost half of the offensive plays are first down this could change how the game is played. The professor gave me an "A" for the paper with the remark "What a unique and clever application of linear programming." Sent a copy to Ralston and two weeks later the Broncos in a game against Kansas City passed on every 1st and 10 and amassed over 600 yards and 42 points. Never heard from the coach but that got me started on developing a computer football game "SEASON FOOTBALL" that is based on NFL statistics. You can play any NFL game and through the Football Hall of Fame I have the statistics for every Super Bowl team going back to 1967. Have kept it up to date now for the past 20 years and the game has correctly predicted the winner for the past 20 Super Bowls. Never had the guts to bet with it though.

An interesting event happened in the class I took on statistics. During one class I could see that some students were having difficulty with some of the math. After class one day, I asked some of them if they wanted some help. They did and I then started to work some problems on the board. I quickly discovered that these Master degree students could not do simple algebra problems: transferring across the equal sign for example. It was hopeless and the my first inkling that our high schools were not doing a very good job, in math at least. Later at VPI this was amply borne out.

The family really enjoyed Boulder. We had a great house up near the mountains. Only Johnny and Duffy were not with us anymore. The kids learned to ski and we made a number of camping trips to the nearby mountains. Janelle finished up her college work at the University graduating with a teaching degree. Jimmy went for one year at Boulder after one year at Virginia Tech. The rest of the brood went to local schools. Joe really thrived there and was always hiking in the mountains right near the house. When we first moved in, we had to buy some new furniture (the first time in many years) and with this buy the salesman talked us into a red recliner. It is different than a Lazy Boy in that the whole chair goes back with the seat and back always at a 90 degree angle. The good Lord was watching out for us because this chair played a very important role many years later, as you will see.

As I discovered, civilian life can be difficult. In the Navy, you never had to worry about a job only where the next duty station was going to be. In civilian life it seemed I was always looking for the next job. Civil Defense money ran out and again I was out of work. I sold some insurance not very successfully but was able to get a contract with the Denver Civil Defense Office for $100 per day any day I wanted to work. The task was not very exciting, analyzing shelter survey reports, but it paid the rent and put food on the table. I worked 4 days a week and spent the fifth day looking for a full time job. I was able to keep my office at the University to do this searching.

JOB SEARCHING

I learned a few tricks while job searching. One of these was to put your a resume in an odd shaped envelope. My resume was 5x8, so the envelope was not the usual size. It stood out. Another tactic is not to respond to advertised jobs by the deadline. Wait about a month and then respond. By that time, the search committee would be looking at the five or so finalists and they would still look at your late entry. It worked as I got a lot of interviews with companies like Coors Beer, the City of Boulder and such. Each time I would send a resume to a company, I would have my secretary find out who the boss was and I would send a letter directly to him bypassing personnel. Most Presidents do not have that much to do and they will usually read such a letter and respond if the resume interests them.

This went on for almost 6 months, the longest period of unemployment since I was 13 years old. The Navy retired pay helped a lot but we were slowly getting in a tight pinch. With no job offers in sight, I began to look at Federal jobs since most of my experience was with Uncle Sam. One day as I was about to sign a letter to the Nuclear Regulatory office in Denver, the name of the boss rang a bell - E. Morris Howard. Could it be the same Morris Howard who once was my electrical engineer at NAVFAC? So I picked up the phone and soon was reminiscing with Morry about the old days at Navy. When he heard I was looking for a job, he invited me to Denver for lunch the next day. At that lunch he told me he could offer me a GS14 in his office but he was moving his office to Fort Worth. I was still welcome to go to Texas but he told me to sit tight and he would see what else was available with the NRC.

Morry called a few days later and told me that there was a GS15 slot open in Chicago that required a civil engineer. It was for the Chief of the Construction Inspection Branch This position had been open for a year and he thought he could get me an interview with the Office Director. So within a few weeks I was on my way to Chicago, actually Glen Ellyn, to interview for this open position. In the interview, I told the Director that my nuclear skills were a bit rusty.

He said not to worry, he needed a manager. Apparently, he thought that I was that manager and he offered me the position.

Important point. Every job that I have had in the civilian world except for VPI, was through someone I had previously known . When you are looking for a job, make sure your friends and acquaintances know about it. Since this was my only offer, I had to accept. So during the summer of 1975, I packed my gear and left for Glen Ellyn to start a new job. Leaving Mom and the kids was one of the hardest things I have ever done since I did not know exactly when I would be back or when the family could join me.

GLEN ELLYN - NUCLEAR REGULATORY COMMISSION (1975 - 1976)

Upon arriving in the area, I was able to find a rooming house to live in and then reported for work on a Monday morning. When I went to the Director's office, he greeted me warmly and introduced me to my immediate supervisor a roly-poly guy named Hunnicutt. We became very good friends. They both warned me that I had a very tough initial personnel problem. Remember that this job had been open for a year and there were at least three men in my branch who were GS14s and eligible for my position. Here was an outsider who got their job. At least three men were very unhappy campers.

I put myself in their position and gave some thought of how to handle this situation. After getting somewhat organized in my new office, I asked the secretary to tell the seven engineers in my branch that we would have a staff meeting after lunch. As they entered the conference room, I could see that most of them were not a happy group. So I introduced myself and gave a brief overview of my background. Then I said something like "If I was one of you men, I would be mad as hell to see an outsider taking this job. But don't blame me. I was selected for it by your supervisors. They must have thought that none of you were qualified for this job. I do not know how long I will be here but I promise you that before I leave with your help and hard work, we will make sure that you are qualified the next time a job like this one opens up. Later on, I will sit down with each of you to get acquainted and help you plan for your next career move." There was a visible change in their attitudes and they all seemed to accept me as their new boss as I shook each man's hand. Apparently the word got around the office because the next day I met the Director in the hallway and he looked at me in amazement with the following statement "What in the world did you say to those guys? They all seem very happy." I told him what I had said and he just walked away shaking his head. He was a golfer, so we became great friends.

The responsibility of my section was to inspect nuclear power plants under construction. I made it a point to go on inspection trips with each of my inspectors. I admitted to them that they knew a lot more about what they were doing than I did but I asked for their help to become knowledgeable. These trips were fun and a great learning experience. A nuclear plant under construction is an awesome sight, like building the great pyramids. Hundreds of thousands of yards of concrete go into a plant and during the height of construction, there are about 3000 workers on site. Our job was to make sure that all specifications were met. I remember one instance as we were walking past an area with thousands of rebar set for a massive concrete pour.

I noticed one area near a tunnel and said to the contractor's rep "There's a rebar missing over there." He looked where I was pointing and said "How do you figure that?" "It's not balanced on both sides" I replied. We went to the field office and sure enough I was right. My stock really went up on that site with the contractor and my own inspectors. It was just luck that I saw that. **Rebar photo below.**

My interest and knowledge of computers also helped me win more support of my guys. I bought a HP calculator that had a 49 step programmable feature. 49 steps is not much but that was the best you could get at the time. At the end of construction, the containment shell had to pass a pressure test. The containment structure is the large structure you see at a plant with a slight curve at the top. It is designed to contain any radioactivity should there be a nuclear accident. The nuclear reactor and other vessels are inside this shell. The shell has sensors in five or six levels and information from this instrumentation is fed to a main frame computer. This test takes several days and it takes time for the final results to come back to the site from a the central computer. I was able to program my little calculator to solve just one level at a time. My results were available in minutes and not hours. Everybody thought I was nuts but my answers were the same as the main frame results. Based on this, NRC had every office equipped with the more sophisticated HP with tape driven memories and 256 step programs. It was a real challenge to program all this into only 49 steps.

An alarming incident happened while I was in Chicago. Jimmy called me from San Diego. He had taken off for the West Coast with his motorcycle and guitar to seek adventure. He had been arrested in San Diego and charged with car theft. All a big mistake but he was in the county jail. Captain Merdinger, my old boss from NCEL, lived near San Diego and I called and asked him to bail Jimmy out and keep him until I could get there. The good Lord provided me with a training trip to San Diego at the same time Jimmy was due to be arraigned. It seemed that Jimmy was hitch hiking and was picked up by a guy driving a pickup truck. They stopped along the beach that night and the driver went to sleep on the beach. Jimmy decided to sleep in the back of the truck. Next morning he was awakened by the cops and charged with stealing the truck. It was a stolen vehicle and the driver that stole the truck had hot wired it. Apparently Jimmy did not notice that there were no keys in the truck.

At Jimmy's arraignment after the charges were read, I raised my hand and the Judge recognized me. I said something like "Your honor, I am the father of James and I am here from Chicago. He is a naive young man but he would never steal anything. He has never been in trouble before and if you release him into my custody, I will make sure he will stay out of trouble." The judge looked at me for a few minutes and then said "It is difficult for me to believe that anyone can be that naive but I will release him to your custody with a one year probation. If he ever gets in trouble in San Diego again, these charges will be brought against him." Bang went the gavel. Jimmy was free. Put him on a bus to Oakland to stay with Gary. I told him to stay out of San Diego.

After only a few months at Glen Ellyn, I decided I did not want to move the family there so I began to look for a job at NRC headquarters in Bethesda, Maryland. The Office of Inspection and Enforcement had a new boss, one of McNamara's whiz kids, who wanted to improve office operations. He set up an evaluation office and was looking for some bright young engineers to staff this office. My boss recommended me even though I was not some young kid. Mr. Volgenau talked to me and he asked me to be on the team. So I became a special analyst and was on my way back to the D.C. area. It was nice being a civil servant instead of a military officer. As a civilian got a lot or perks that military do not get when moving. For example the NRC paid for us to spend a week in the DC area to look for a house. We found a place we could afford in Manassas. Our old Hillbrook house we could no longer afford. It had increased in price by a factor of 2 in the 3 years we were in Colorado. We flew Joyce and Joe out to Dulles and they stayed with Johnny and Linda until we arrived. By that time all the rest had flown the coop except for Jean and she wanted to stay with her friend in Boulder to finish high school. That was a big mistake but we let her stay.

MANASSAS - THE NRC (1976-1981)

When we first came to Virginia in 1962, Manassas was a little sleepy crossroads town. When we moved there it had grown. I had to drive 32 miles one-way to Bethesda to the NRC headquarters. Our study team consisted of me as the senior, and two young guys who had graduated from the Air Force Academy. They were sharp and we made a good team. Later we had several other recent college graduates join us. Our job was to analyze the Office of Inspection and Enforcement and recommend how it could be improved. This study took about 18 months and in the end we changed the office operations in a very significant way. One of the major changes was the placement of resident inspectors at reactor sites. **Received my 25 year service pin** at the NRC. **Picture at right.**

While in Manassas, Mom began attending a charismatic prayer meeting on Monday nights in the Catholic Church. This was an ecumenical group of Protestants and Catholics, led my a Catholic couple. She loved it but I couldn't go because there was Monday night football. Could not give that up. Mom continued to tell me about this prayer meeting where you could really sing the praise songs and listen to testimonies and receive teachings from the Bible. Well one Monday night game was not too thrilling, so I went with her. Changed my life. During my entire life I hardly ever missed Sunday mass nor had ever studied the Bible. At these prayer meetings the Bible was opened up to me. Here I was 55 years old and I never had been told by any priest that I must be born again. See John 3:3. We were both born again in that prayer group and have since diligently sought God. We only wish this had happened sooner and a number of things in our lives would have been different.

When the office study ended I was offered the position of Chief of the NRC inspector training division. This division had a number of courses that each inspector had to take at Bethesda and in Chattanooga, Tennessee. The Chattanooga courses were on the TVA reactor simulators. While in Glen Ellyn I had taken the BWR (Boiling Water) and PWR (Pressurized Water) reactor courses. I had this job from 1978 to 1981. I applied for other higher level jobs that came up but was not selected for anything else since office politics seemed to be the criteria for selection and I was not one of the inner circle.

During this time, the Three Mile Island event occurred. The training division was not directly involved in this affair but one of my instructors had been an operator there and knew how the plant operated. This was a PWR reactor designed by B&W that had a once through condenser. This type of design did not have the same margin of safety as a PWR designed by Westinghouse. When my instructor arrived about 8:30 that morning and looked at the data coming in from Three Mile Island, he loudly proclaimed to Vic Stello, the man in charge at headquarters "Tell them to get that emergency water back on right now!" Stello said they had to wait for more data to come in. The instructor then replied "My God, you are stomping on the mice and the

elephant is running out the door!" He was proved right and if his advice had been followed, most of the catastrophe would have been averted. He proved out one of my management tenets - Pay attention to the little guy, he may know more than the top dogs. **My office at NRC HQ to right.**

Because of the numerous trips that we had to make to Chattanooga, I recommended that my whole division should be based there. This move was finally approved in late 1980 and we moved there in early 1981. Our new quarters were really great. We had one whole floor of a new office building and we now had great classrooms and spacious offices. Mine must have been 40 by 40 feet with a view over looking a par 3 golf course. Mom came down on a trip once and we decided that we did not want to move there. So I began to look elsewhere in NRC. Then one day I saw an ad in the Retired Officers' magazine for a professorship at Virginia Tech. A Ph.D. was not essential.

I called Bud Devens, the ad writer, a retired Army officer and West Pointer of about my vintage, and asked him what the position required. He asked me what I had to offer. He liked what he heard and asked me to send him a resume. Within a few weeks Bud invited me down for an interview. I was able to combine this trip with one to Chattanooga. At Tech I talked mostly with

Bud, met a few of the other profs and had a short session with Dr. Torgensen, the Engineering Dean. It all seemed to go well and I went on to Tennessee. While in Chattanooga Bud called and told me the job was mine if I wanted it. I told him I would stop on the way back to Virginia. It turned out Bud was a golfer and the father of eight too. When I left Chattanooga it was hot and humid. At Blacksburg it was hot but not too humid. Played golf with Bud at the country club and told him I would let him know after I talked with Mom. When I got back to Manassas, it was hot and humid again. This weather difference played a part in my decision. The offer was for $27,500 per year and my current NRC salary was $55,000. So this needed some thought.

The cost of living was lower in Blacksburg than in Manassas and I would get my full Navy retired pay. The VPI job is really only a nine month job and the work travel would only be minutes instead of hours. With all the kids gone (we innocently thought) our income would be fine for only two people. So we decided to take the teaching job and I submitted my resignation from the NRC. The next day a huge figure loomed in my doorway and it was the godfather like figure of my NRC super boss, Vic Stello. He said he could find me a job right there and he pleaded with me not to leave. I told him that I had applied for other jobs but I was apparently too old for them. He said it was all a mistake and he would find me a job with a promotion. I told him that my decision was firm. He could not understand that. Driving only a mile to the office verses the 32 on the Beltway was reason enough.

THE VPI YEARS (1981-1994)

Always enjoyed teaching so I really looked forward to this new job at Virginia Tech, as an Associate Professor. Almost all of my teaching and lecturing experience was with people about my own age and engineers like me. The Naval Academy was with first year students but the academy was all military and discipline was tight. I was not sure what it would be like teaching college level students, both men and women.

Some time later, I found out that there had been sixty plus applicants for this position and yet I was offered the job only a week after my interviews. As chairman of several hiring committees later on, I found that we usually required the applicants to give a lecture to the department staff. They did not ask me to do this and I asked Bud Devins why I did not do this. He said that once he talked to me, he decided that this would not be necessary. The rest of the staff seem to readily accept this new Prof. as we met several weeks before class started. So I nervously awaited my first classroom experience. As a golfer, I applied for all the 8 a.m. classes to leave some afternoons free for playing golf.

The Engineering Fundamental classrooms were different than what one usually sees in a college classroom. There were 28 drawing room tables for the 28 students as one of the courses was engineering drawing, the very subject I had taught at the Academy. In the front of the room was a podium for the instructor and behind this was a full wall of black boards.

As I entered the class room that first morning at 7:55 I could see that most of the students were seated and looking curiously at this old man as he entered the room. I wrote my name and phone number on the board, handed out the syllabus to each student and then turned to survey the class. About one third of the class were women, a new teaching experience for me since all my former students had been men. After looking at each of these young and nice looking students, I said something like this: **Prof ID at left.**

Good morning ladies and gentlemen. Welcome to your engineering class. Most of you look a little nervous and wonder what to expect here. Let me assure you that the objective of this class is not to fail anyone. We are as anxious as you are to see that you succeed. The country needs good engineers. My name and phone number are on the board - that is pronounced LeDoo I am giving you my phone number and you may call me at night if you have any questions or need help with a problem. That invitation is good until 11 p.m. after that you will probably not get a coherent response.

Today you are embarking on a professional career and we expect you to act like one in this classroom at least. We expect that you dress accordingly - no short shorts, no cutoffs, no hats in class. Neat and clean. Period.

Passing this class is really simple: attend class every day and do all the homework. Do that and understand what you are doing will guarantee success. We do not grade on a curve nor do we inflate grades. You will received the grade that reflects your effort. This may mean that you may get a "C". You may never have heard of such a grade but it stands for average. Based on past experience in a class of 28, about 5 or so will receive As", about the same number will earn "Bs", 2 or 3 may get "Ds" or "Fs" and the rest will get the "C". I realize that most if not all of you were "A" students in high school but accept the fact that you are now competing against many top students and that the average among such a group is still a "C". However, since we do not grade on a curve, everyone of you could earn an "A".

How, your may ask, can a former top high school student fail such a class? Generally from lack of work, not attending class, not doing your own homework, not getting help when you need it. Let me emphasize that I am on your side. You are about the age of my own eight kids and I am here to help you succeed. I can help but I can not do your work for you. Most of you have found high school easy, In fact some students tell me it was boring. You may not know how to study or budget your time. It takes about 60 hours per week to do all that you must do: class time is about 20 hours per week and it usually averages 2 hours of outside homework for each classroom hour. Later on I will show you how to budget your time to accomplish this. My budget advice includes time to play and relax and do your laundry. Yes, your Mom is not hers to do that anymore, so include it in your schedule. Many of you probably had part time jobs at a fast food place and earned a few dollars per hour. If you feel the urge to goof off let me inform you how much per hour you will earn getting your engineering degree. You will earn about $1.5 million more in your lifetime over your friends who do not go to college. If your friend becomes a plumber, he is *excepted. Divide the 60 hours per week for 4 years of classes into the $1.5 million and you will discover you are earning over $150 per hour.*

This first year of engineering study will introduce you to all the various engineering disciplines. In the Spring you will be asked to select your engineering specialty. This is an important decision but you should not lose any sleep over it. Looking at me you may think that I have been teaching for a long time. The truth is that I am not an academician but have recently joined this staff after 35 years as a professional engineer. I hope that this experience will benefit you as I will bring my experience in the real world to what we teach you. Remember what I told you about the "C" grade? One of the best engineers I ever worked with was a "C" student from Cal Poly. Sometimes "C" students have to work hard for the "C" but because of this work, they remember more than the "A" student who finds college work easy. Now back to your choice of engineering specialty. In the real world, once you have been hired, your boss could care less what type of engineer you are or what school you went to and will assign you a job that has to be done and that may be out of your specialty. You just have to do it. So when you select optional courses, select as many as you can outside your field. Be as general as you can.

You were given a course syllabus. Look it over and keep pace with the reading assignments. You will note that you have 2 midterms and one final. The midterms are department tests and the final is one that I will write. In addition you will have a term project that I again will devise. It will cover most of the knowledge that I hope you will take from this course into future courses. One last policy that I have. If you pass my final, which also covers all the important material in the course, you will pass this course no matter what your other grades have been. The grade may be a "D" but that is passing. Any questions?

The rest of the period was devoted to having each student introduce themselves to the class and then we covered what math they would need and a general overview of the course.

This first quarter course was a problem solving course with problems selected from various fields of engineering. I had graduated from high school almost 40 years before and I expected that these engineering students would be as well prepared as I was when I went to the University of California as a freshman in the Navy V12 program. What a shock, when I discovered that the math background for most of the students was woefully lacking in the basics of geometry, trigonometry, and analytical geometry. Even their algebra was not too good. Remember Boulder? To help them is this subject, I gave a series of math review classes at night on a volunteer basis. Every night the class room was packed with mine and other profs' students.

Later on, when grading their term papers, I discovered that their writing skills were worse than their math ability. Inventive spelling, poor sentence and paragraph structure was evident for most of the students. How could this be? What were they doing for the past 12 years? This led me to investigate what was going on in our present day high schools. What I found out was appalling. This led me to the writing of many op-ed pieces that have been published in various newspapers and other publications. I am thinking of putting them all in another book titled "One Man's Point of View".

I really enjoyed teaching these young adults. The rewards of seeing most of them overcome their relatively poor education was greater than any pay that I could receive. Many students claimed in their evaluations that my help and encouragement gave them the incentive to keep trying. Some students gave up engineering and transferred to other colleges. One particular student comes to mind: Ed Lee (Chinese American). He should have transferred but continued to knock his head against a wall.

Ed's father was the head waiter at Trader's Vic in DC and insisted that Ed should be an engineer. He barely passed the freshman courses and I insisted he take a vocational evaluation test given by VPI. His engineering aptitude was a low 10 percent. He was very artistic and spoke 4 languages. I advised him to give up on engineering and study courses that would lead to a State Department type of career. He finally gave up in the 3rd year since he never could pass the statics course.

Another example of the typical "feel good" type of help given in many public schools was a young man who failed the first midterm. His grade was about 20 based mostly on the fact that he spelled his name correctly. When a student fails a test, I ask them to come in to discuss it to try and find out why they failed. This young man did not even try the first problem on the test. There were only 3 problems in this 50 minute test. I asked him why he did not try to do this problem. He claimed he did not know how to do it. I asked to see his textbook since a similar problem was in the reading assignments. It was obvious that this book had never even been opened. I pointed out that clear instructions were printed at the top of the page, about 3 sentences. He then told me it would take him too long to read those sentences. I turned the exam around and said "Read it to me now". He tried but could not read those instructions. He could not really read, thus the unopened book. There was no way this student could pass this or any course at college. As he left the office he said "I still feel good about myself." What a triumph for the "feel good" philosophy.

Later on in my investigation of public school education, a school principal told me, rather proudly, that "the purpose of schools is not education but socialization." Then I discovered that most schools "taught" reading by the "whole word" or "look say" method. This is educational malpractice of major proportions. This so called method can only cover about 400 words per year or about 5000 in 12 years of school. The dictionary has over 500,000 words. When I was in grammar school in the 1930s we were taught the ABCs. Phonics was not a known word then but that is how we learned to read. In the second grade I was getting books from the public library and always reading one. Still do. It is obvious that one must first **learn to read** so that he can then **read to learn**.

Another story about this feel good philosophy was about one of my men students from New York. He was in one of my 8 a.m. classes and showed up for the first few days. Then he was absent for a few days. I phoned him to see if he was sick. He wasn't and told me he would be in class the next day. He was. But then he began to miss class. I called him and told him to come into the office. When confronted he told me this story. *"When I was in high school, I was in several different clubs and social activities kept me up till 11 at night. Then I did my homework, if any. I am still active in many things and my homework here takes 4 or 5 hours to do. I have to sleep in"* He looked at me expectantly as if I could do something for him. I reminded him it takes 60 hours per week to do the engineering curriculum and he better give up his outside activities. He never did and was the only student I ever had who ended up with a zero QSA. At the end of this quarter, he told me he would be back next year. He never did. I assume his father finally woke up and realized his son was a loser.

The girls in my classes were better writers than the boys and seemed to pay more attention to their required work. One sad story concerns one young black women who needed a lot of help. I spent at least several hours each week with her and even went to her dorm room to help her with her computer. In spite of all that help, she failed the course. I received an angry phone call from her mother berating me for failing her "A" student daughter. When she finally ran out of steam, I suggested she talk to her daughter about all the help I gave her. Then I suggested that she confront her high school math teacher since her math skills were sadly lacking. She received good grades in high school in spite of her lack of knowledge. She did have great social skills.

Self esteem is based on individual accomplishment not on some ill deserved pat on the back, unless the pat is low enough. One of my objectives in each class was to give term projects that required some effort but completion offered true accomplishment and true self esteem. Back in the days before we had desk top computers, the students had to do their programming by using punch cards which then went to a main frame computer. There was only two runs a day to find and correct errors, a most frustrating ordeal. At the end of one semester, on the last day for completion of the programming problem, a student came in to my office to get his card deck. He was really down hearted since he did not expect success. I handed him the deck and printout and congratulated him on a job well done. He just beamed all over and said he wanted to show this to his folks. Many times before we had computer graphics I would get the same reaction to a drawing project that was well done and they took these home to show the folks too. Self esteem is earned not bestowed. Why can't the public schools see that? A recent news article wrote about the effect of grade inflation. Some 40 percent of the students earned "As" when only 10 years ago the percentage was 21 percent. The "C" grade has disappeared. The excuse given was to help students get to the college of their choice. The shock comes when they arrive at the college and find they can't do the work. .

Remember our dress code? No hats in class. One morning, George Lux, arrived in class about 5 minutes early. There in the front row was a young man with his hat on - backwards naturally. George told him to take his hat off. The student said that class had not started yet and therefor he was on his time. George walked over, picked up the student's book bag, and then walked to the door and threw it out in the corridor. When the student went to retrieve it, George locked the door and started class. He paid no attention to the student who tried to get back in the class. Needless to say, there was no more hat wearing in Lux's classes.

Prof. LeDoux on the left.

One of my girl students had what I can only describe as a dual personality, like the Three Faces of Eve movie. Most days she would be nicely groomed and acted in a very normal fashion. Then she would come in looking like something the cat refused to drag in and in this state would disrupt the class with her actions. I had to tell her to sit down and be quiet and I would talk to her after class. She finally demanded a transfer to another instructor and Bill Rogers was the lucky guy. He couldn't control her either.

These thirteen years passed swiftly and pleasantly. I had over 1000 students during this time and received many letters from them on how I helped them. One particular story I got second hand. At some senior party a girl remarked to some in the room that she would not be there if it had not been for Professor LeDoux's help and encouragement. **Above a note from a Ms.Kim.** Things like that are what I call intrinsic rewards.

To summarize this period, a quote from Professor Devins recommendation for my tenure is appropriate. " Professor LeDoux is a dedicated, enthusiastic, hard working teacher and advisor who challenges his students and receives top performance in return. Student evaluations in all of his sections for the past six years rate him 3.56 on a scale of 1.00 (low) to 4.00 (high), placing him consistently at the top of all College of Engineering faculty. He has been the faculty advisor to over one hundred freshmen each year and takes this responsibility most seriously, spending countless hours in individual counseling while carefully monitoring each student's academic progress. His door is always open to his students, with whom he has developed an exceptional rapport. Students sense his intense personal interest in them as individuals and know that he often goes far out of his way to help a student overcome problems of every nature." It goes on to cover my contribution to computer programming and other work. This, I am sure, led to the receipt of Emeritus status when I retired in 1994.

THE RED RECLINER

It was during this period that the red recliner played an important and sometimes funny role in our lives. About 1985 Betty was diagnosed with degenerative arthritis of the lower spine. The doctor suggested that she should sleep in a recliner. Lo and behold, the red chair fit the bill perfectly. A standard recliner would not since the back angle changes. The red chair has a permanent 90 degree angle.

When I was on my California trip in 1988, Betty fell off the front steps while trying to call our border Collie. She just leaned over and fell. Both arms were broken. She was alone, and the Ramble Road house was quite isolated. She could not get up. Our nearest neighbor was over 100 feet away and the houses were separated by a large hedge. Fortunately, the wife was going to the bathroom and faintly heard Betty calling for help. When the emergency people came, Pepper put his paws on Betty's chest and would not let anyone touch her. Janelle was called and rushed over to solve that problem. She went to the hospital with Mom and stayed there while they took care of her. About an hour later, the orthopedist finally arrived. Janelle had been out of the room for a few minutes and when she returned, she did not think they had done enough for her mother. She turned to the Doctor and exclaimed " Why don't you do something?" The doctor turned to her and patiently said "Well, I just got here!!" When they finally finished with getting her stabilized, they put her in a room and were going to operate on both arms the next day. I was called in California and got the next plane home.

After getting home and checking on Mom, I went home and brought the red chair and its footstool over to the hospital. They were very nice about letting us bring it up to her room and setting it up. After the surgery she had both arms in casts and the right arm had a plate and several screws in it. She was then allowed to stay in her chair during the day. That night, the nurse wanted to put her in the bed and Janelle had to exclaim "No. no, she sleeps in that chair!!" While she was in the hospital, I slept in the bed and stayed with her most of the time. The girls spared me quite often.

An interesting footnote to this episode was the hospital bill, about $6500 for the week. Since we were on Champus (the military medical program), they paid the bill but only allowed $2500. The hospital had to accept that as full payment since they are a teaching hospital. I have always wondered about people who were not covered by Champus. Was the $6500 a fair charge?

That red chair has been in hospitals more than most people, 5 times I think. Three times at Montgomery and twice in Roanoke when Betty had heart surgery.

I went to Blacksburg in 1981 and we did not move until 1982 since Joe still had a year left at Stonewall Jackson High. He was a BMOC and did not want to switch schools so I drove every weekend from August until June. Rented a little basement apartment in Blacksburg and roughed it out that year. Mom came down in June to look for a place to live. We could not find anything that suited us especially since we needed space for the baby grand piano. On our last day the real estate agent met us at the Ramble Road house as it had just came on the market. The property was great but the house was a mess except for the dining and living rooms. I did not think Mom was interested because the kitchen and bath rooms were disaster areas. Also where would we put the baby grand? It turned out she was interested and we bought it for $82,500. We spent a lot more fixing up the kitchen and bath rooms. Eventually we added a big bedroom wing and later added a wing to the dining room area. We were able to sell the Manassas house in two weeks even in a depressed market. The baby grand sale is a story of how the Lord works in our lives if we pray about it. See Proverbs 3:6.

We bought this Kawai piano when they first came on the market for $1600. We found a dealer who would sell it on consignment. We would net $3200. So we advertised and waited. A number of people looked at it and one bar owner made an offer but we did not want our piano in a bar. One day a couple came from a town almost 100 miles away and looked at it. She played a few notes and there was some strange sounds. When the top was opened, some pennies were found that affected some notes. After they were removed it played great. They were a Christian couple and needed a piano for their ministry. They asked what we wanted for it and we asked them to make an offer. Apparently they had been saving for two years and had saved $3200. Coincidence? I don't think so. They prayed for a good piano they could afford and we prayed that we could sell it where it would find a good home. They paid us $1600 right then and two weeks later came back with a truck and the other $1600. His ways are higher than ours.

During this time my youngest son Joe was going to Cornell under a Navy ROTC scholarship. We still had to pay for room and board that was almost the same as full costs at VPI. I had the privilege of **swearing Joe into the Navy. Picture at right.**

The Ramble Road property was right near Tech and yet very private. It is almost a game reserve with deer, rabbits, squirrels, birds and other animals. We thought we would finally be alone since all the kids had flown the coop. But Janelle, Judy, Jeannie and for short periods Joe lived with us. A bit crowded but still great. My schedule, always 8 a.m. classes, allowed me to play golf at least 3 times a week. This has been the longest time we have ever lived anywhere. Three of the girls settled in the area. Joyce moved later to Northern Virginia where John lived since his Vietnam tour.. Joe is now a professor at Georgia Tech. Jim and Jeff are Californians.

During these years in Blacksburg, two other events took place that need to be noted: the 1992 reunion and the 50th anniversary party.

THE 1992 FAMILY REUNION

Over the years the family scattered and we have not been together since we went to Colorado in 1973. So Janelle, the master organizer, set up the reunion and somehow got everyone to attend. She even invited a local reporter, Kathleen Wilson, to come. Kathleen wrote a column for the Roanoke Times titled "Mingling" about various local events. It was a great time for all and I think we had about 35 people here. Duffy and Jimmy came from California. Kathleen stayed all day and her column is reproduced here with a few of our additions to it to make it complete. When she wrote her last Mingling column, she said that her favorite column and time spent was with the LeDoux tribe. Her column is on the next page. We took some pictures of the kids in poses from when they were little. The girls could hold the little boys back then, but as you can see from the photos, they find it very difficult to hold six footers like Joe. See the comparison between 1967 and 1992 on the next page.

Sadly, about 2 years later Kathleen died on the operating table for what was supposed to be a non critical operations. She was like one of the family and we miss her

These are the two photographs mentioned above. The first was taken about 1967 when Joe was three. The one below was taken at the reunion to try to duplicate the first one. My how the boys have grown! Jean too. Janelle is lost in the 1992 photo.

THE EIGHT IN 1967

Kathleen's column is printed on the next page.

Confessions at a family reunion

John and Betty LeDoux's eight children haven't been together in 21 years.

The clan last gathered in 1971 — the year Johnny, the oldest son, came home from Vietnam.

Today he's 42.

But at 1:08 p.m. on Saturday, June 6, Janelle, 38, was able to

MINGLING
KATHLEEN WILSON

shout for the first time "The Le-Douxs are all here!"

It was quite an adventure.

With grandchildren, in-laws, significant others and one reporter, Betty found herself cooking dinner for 27. She claims it's not that big a deal, as she cooked for 10 when the kids were all at home.

Papa John LeDoux recently retired from Virginia Tech's engineering faculty. Though he and Betty have lived in their Blacksburg home a stone's throw from the Tech campus on Ramble Road for 11 years now, John laughs as he points out they've only been there alone for two years.

Jimmy, 37, who hasn't been home from California in 10 years, was introducing himself to nieces and nephews he's never met.

He started a LeDoux family tradition that the youngest son, Joe, 28, carries on: The Ramble Rag, the family tabloid.

Picking on mom was so popu-

PLEASE SEE **MINGLING**/6

Mingling

FROM PAGE 1

lar she not only warranted the lead story in each issue, but also "The Mom Page." Most of the stories were devoted to Betty's travails in the kitchen.

When she left an oven mitt in the oven, The Ramble Rag's headline read "Mom Makes Mittloaf!"

Other highlights include: "Blender Attacks Spatula: Janelle Blamed!"; "Janelle Murders Mouse!"; "It's War: Mom Attacks Flies"; "Jeanie Wins $10,000"; and "Family Football Pool To Be Computerized."

As soon as the LeDouxs were all were seated for dinner — at tables scattered throughout three rooms of John and Betty's house — the phone rang.

"Now *that's* classic," said Jean, 32.

The dinner conversation was solid gold, with The Eight Originals shouting, "I have a confession!"

For example, Janelle remembers being 14 and going to the movies with a 19-year-old. Papa John went into the theater and found the two of them necking.

"I snuck up behind them and announced loudly 'It's time to go home, Janelle.'" Today they can laugh about it.

Jeffrey, 41, — they call him Duffy — had confessions involving toilet-papering the neighbors' homes. He's proudest of the times he TP'd in broad daylight ... while the neighbors were cooking out in the back yard.

Today he's a wholesale florist, prompting his brother-in-law Bob to comment, "And you're still in the decorating business."

In a family with eight children, it shouldn't be a surprise that toilet paper played such a titanic role. Jimmy actually made a documentary film in high school about how to TP a house.

"He got an A-," Papa John said proudly.

After dinner the LeDouxs reenacted the last time The Eight Originals were photographed 27 years ago — with black-and-white film.

This Keystone Cops effort put the tallest and the youngest, Joe, on the knee of his considerably smaller, but older sister Janelle.

The LeDouxs reminded me some of the Kennedys. OK, so they aren't Irish. They live in a house not on a compound. And maybe there aren't any sailboats around.

But there are four boys. And four girls. There were 10 cars in the driveway. And 10 grandchildren running around. A football lay in the front yard, lawn dart equipment nearby. That Friday they played football, volleyball and baseball.

"We're a crazy family, aren't we?" Janelle's 9-year-old, Shana, said with a smile.

A plaque in the house probably best sums up the glue that has bound this group over the years. It reads: "Fruit Of The Spirit: Love, Joy, Peace, Patience, Kindness, Goodness, Faithfulness, Gentleness, Self-Control."

THE 50ᵀᴴ WEDDING ANNIVESARY

In 1998, Janelle again organized a party for our 50ᵗʰ. She rented the ballroom at a local motel and invited everyone who knew us from the Church and from my gang at VPI. It was a lot of fun and everyone seemed to enjoy the evening. A few photos from the night are in this story. All the kids had the opportunity to roast their parents and they really did an outstanding job. It was very funny how they remembered some crazy times. Mom and I had a few minutes of rebuttal. We also said our vows over again with Pastor Vince presiding. We both stated we would do it all over again, given the chance. We can both honestly say that our marriage and relationship is better than ever, We are best friends and lovers still. We had a rough time in the 70s due to my juvenile actions but Betty was kind enough and wise enough to forgive me and we went on from there. The picture below is the **family at the 50ᵗʰ** anniversary party. Now I know how Abraham got to be the father of many nations. **The second shot is Mom and Dad being roasted by kids.**

POST VPI

Since retiring from Tech I have been active in politics for the Republican Party. Attended three state conventions, been a precinct captain, and ran for the school board. I have also been active in trying to reverse the illiteracy that is rampant in our public schools. I have written a number of quest columns in local newspapers on this subject and a few on abortion. One column was about the 4th of July. This activity has brought me into contact with many people throughout the United States. There are now some trends that could lead to the teaching of phonics in the public schools again.

In 2001 we sold the Ramble Road house after 3 years of haggling with a developer for a tidy sum and did not have to move for a year. We were able to design and build a new house in the upper hills of Blacksburg and moved into it in May of 2002. Life came full cycle when I was able to help the contractor build the house from the foundation to the roof. Drove a few thousand nails and saw every stick put in place. It is great house for betty with all the essentials on one floor. We enjoy the two car garage and I have a nice little office. Never had the chance to do my specialty, driving stakes in the ground. This house also has our second Murphy bed in the upstairs sitting room. Mom saw a program on TV where they were installing a Murphy Bed. So through this program we were able to locate the manufacturer and ordered one for the new house. This one was much better than our first back in Long Beach in 1948.

New article when I ran for school board. Lost

THE GREAT GAME OF GOLF

You are probably aware of the number of times I mentioned the game of golf in this story. It has really played an important role in my life and helps me keep relatively healthy at age 78 going on 79. I still walk but now use a pull cart for the 18 holes.

I taught Joe in Colorado when he was about 8 years old. Made him play with a 5 iron and a putter for about 2 years before he got other clubs. He is still a great iron player and we had some wonderful matches over the years. Now that Johnny plays and Joyce and Rick have started and the grandsons Matt and John have also started, I thought I would finish this story about my golfing life. Grandson John has become a really good player and is now in college studying the business aspects of the game. He gives me credit as his first teacher.

I have played a lot of sports both team and individual but golf has to be the best individual sport invented by man. I disagree with Mark Twain who said that golf is a good walk spoiled. It is a sport that can never be truly mastered but provides a challenge and a satisfaction offered by no other sport. It is always played in God's open air and in beautiful settings. It can be truly frustrating but fulfilling at the same time.

At the Naval Academy we were introduced to all sports including golf but I was not interested. My friend and shipmate, Jim Hayes, got me to go one day in Long Beach. I broke 100 that first time and had a few pars and that was it. The game is addicting and it had me good.

When we went to the Academy in 1949 I had plenty of time to play and Mom even took a few lessons. During this time I was a 90s shooter but had times when I played well improving to a mid 80 golfer in a few years and there I was stuck until the lessons in Monterey when I became a high 70 and low 80 golfer.

Golf is a great game for meeting people. It is also reveals character since each golfer essentially is his own referee. I have played with cheaters, club throwers, and those who swear. Most of the time I have met and played with really nice people. My Navy career offered me the opportunity to play over many parts of the world: Guam, Saipan, Australia, New Zealand and in most areas of the United States. The well known courses played: Pebble Beach, Olympic Club, Bay Hill, Riviera, Beverly Hills Country Club, Torry Pines. I've played many others not so famous or expensive but the common thread has been the beauty of them all. At the Beverly Hills club I used a locker next to Gary Cooper.

Career rounds: lowest round was a par 70 at Virginia Tech; won only two noteworthy tournaments - Shot a 73 at Westwood Country Club in Fairfax in a Pentagon affair. The other was a Senior win at Prince William newspaper tournament with a 74; in a Service league at Port Hueneme, came from 3 down with 4 to play to win; played on a Navy team in San Diego and Las Vegas. Career shots: the 110 foot putt in New Zealand; once hit a 3 wood about 300 yards on a California course many years ago; came within an inch of a double eagle at Fort Belvoir with a 4 wood; hit a ball once out from between the roots of a tree to within a foot of the hole for a birdie; have had a number of eagles by pitching in from the fairway or trap. Still play in high 70s and low 80s. Finally shot my age at 74. Just missed by a stroke doing that at age 73. Three putted the 18th an easy par 5. My game has stayed pretty good through these last few years and I now shoot my age most of the time. You other family golfers have some targets to shoot at. Have a great game. Oh yeah, I have had two holes in one - one witnessed and one only I saw. Bud Devins made up this elaborate certificate that started out "Jack LeDoux claims….". Very funny.

PISTOL SHOOTING

A number of times in this story, I mentioned two other sports that I was able to participate in: pistol shooting and bowling. When I was about 9 or 10, my dad taught me how to safely handle both a rifle and a pistol. His one primary instruction was "Don' t ever point a gun at anything or anyone unless you intend to kill them". He was an expert with his 38 Smith & Wesson. While hunting squirrels in the hills one day, I witnessed a remarkable shot. At something over 50 yards, he picked off a squirrel with a single shot. He really taught me how to squeeze the trigger. These lessons really helped me a number of times during my life. Every time I see the movie "The Magnificent Seven" I am reminded of his squirrel shot and the squeezing of a trigger with two scenes in that movie.

During plebe summer at the Academy, we had to qualify with both a pistol and a rifle. My training paid off when I qualified as expert in both weapons earning two medals and ribbons. Based on this, I was made the captain of the Astoria's pistol team and participated in matches in San Diego. At Port Hueneme all officers had to qualify with a 45 to stand Officer of the Day watches. When I went to the range to qualify, a Chief Petty Officer handed me a 45 from a rack. I asked him if I could select my own. He waved his hand toward a rack of about 10 of them. I tested each one for two things: how much did the gun rattle when I shook it and how stiff was the trigger pull. Most 45s are rather loosely assembled and most have too stiff a trigger pull. That's why they have a poor reputation by most military people who would rather throw the gun at an enemy than try to shoot them. I finally found a gun that did not rattle too much and had a pull of about 2 pounds. In the wind at a range of 50 yards, I shot a 95 with most shots in the black nine and ten ring.

The chief was duly impressed and asked me if I would be willing to be the base team officer rep. I accepted. We had another CPO on the team. He was a large man and the 45 pistol was almost lost in his hand. He was a great shot and had participated in the National matches in Ohio. He helped me quite a bit. The one amazing thing he showed me was that if you truly squeezed off a shot, you would see the bullet leave the gun. I though he was kidding but I quickly found out it was true. With copper service ammo, I could see the copper bullet about an inch past the end of the barrel before I blinked.

The matches at San Diego were the National Match format: 50 yards at slow fire (no set time limit to fire the 10 rounds), timed fire (5 shots in 20 seconds) and rapid fire (5 shots in 10 seconds) He taught me to lean into the shot with extended right arm. The recoil would make your arm go up about a foot. The first two were not really a problem but the last was difficult.

The old chief taught me how to absorb the recoil so that your arm would drop back on the target.

You had to start squeezing the trigger when your arm is raised so that you would fire when back on target. You just tried to get your sights somewhere in the black. We used only a one hand grip not like the two hands you now see on TV cop shows. I managed to win several aggregate medals at these matches. The aggregate score was the total for the three types of fire. In some matches we competed against civilians. We were at a disadvantage in these matches since we had to use service ammo and the civilians usually loaded their own ammo with a smaller and more uniform amount of powder. This reduced recoil to almost nothing. Their weapons were also much more precise than the old 45. We did send our 45s to a San Francisco gun smith to make the parts fit better (no rattle) and smooth trigger pull of about 1.5 lbs. I was actually invited to the National matches but could not take the time to go.

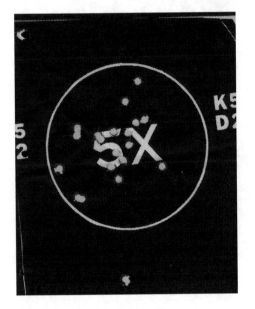

To close out my experience as a pistol shooter, in 1999 I participated in a Citizens Police Academy with the Sheriff's office. It was extremely interesting and educational and after a 40 year span, I was able to shoot a pistol again. They used a Glock type of automatic, very light and small. At the range I was able to put 19 of 20 shots in the center of the man sized target. The 20th shot was just 2 inches below the circle. One of the deputies exclaimed "You shoot better than most of us". **My target is above**. The circle is 6 inches in diameter.

BOWLING

I started bowling when I was about 12 years old. Bowling establishments in those days were really "alleys" and unfit for the gentler sex. The games cost only 10 cents per line and the pins were set by pin boys, who always had a comment on your bowling skills. When I was dating Mom, she was bowling in a league and I would be there if I did not have the duty. Most of the time a team would not have five members show up, so I would pace or take the place of missing bowler. My score did not count but it was good practice.

When we were at Hueneme, I bowled in a base mixed league and averaged about 175-180. That's where I bowled my second 277 for high scratch score for that year. As mentioned before, I also bowled on the Navy base team. We made trips to San Diego and Las Vegas. Except for me all the team members were enlisted men and all were better than me even though I averaged 185 on that team. In one of the many tournaments, I won the All Events trophy with the best score for nine games: team, doubles and singles. In that tournament, I averaged 211 for the 9 games. Also earned patches for picking up most of the splits, even the wide ones.

While at Cheatham we built a new bowling alley for the base, 12 lanes. Do not remember any great games their but I did perfect picking up the 10 pin. I bowled a curve and that pin was difficult for me. One day I had a friend set up the 10 pin for me and I must have practiced that mark about 50 times until I rarely missed that pin. It was also good for picking up the 3-10 split.

While there, I also gave lessons to the wives and kids.

After some 30 years of bowling, the Hueneme time was the last time I ever did any serious bowling.

Accepting   team trophy from the CO

Finally happily retired in 1994 for good.

THE STORY CONTINUES

One of the privileges of being the father of 4 beautiful daughters is dancing at their weddings. These weddings also gave me the opportunity to again wear my Navy evening dress blues. Could still fit into them after over 20 years of retirement. This frustrates my dear wife. I must admit I was proud to wear Navy blue and I still am. .

JOYCE

JANELLE

My granddaughter Dyana really blessed me with the following note on a birthday card "*Papa - I just want to tell you that you I love you very much. You are the most positive male figure that I have had in my life, and I don't think that I have told you enough. Love- Dyana*"

This was another intrinsic reward that money can't buy! Thanks Dy.

I spoke of the trouble that Mom and I had in the 70s so I am closing this story with the only poem I ever wrote. It was to Mom when we got over our problem. No problem is too great that it can't be solved if two people love each other. Pray for wisdom. God will give it to you.

TWO RINGS OF LOVE

Once there were two rings,
One a promise, bright and sparkling
The other, a gift of life and love,
Gifts, endless like perfect circles
Pure like gold of white.

Time passed.
The purity of love remained hidden within
Because the brightness and sparkle dimmed,
As life itself.
A star was lost.

Tighter yet the rings became
Until they burst.
Perfect circles no longer.
In darkness did they hide.

Time passed.
A fearful storm ensued
With dark nights,
Sunless days and rains of tears.

Then a gift from God,
A dawn of understanding,
Blue sky, bright sun, brilliant stars.
Two rings emerge from hiding

Perfect circles once again
Bright with hope
Sparkling with life
Grown now to hold a more perfect love.

Time again will pass
Life will burden still
No longer to dim
The promise of one
Nor the gift of the other.

Jack to Betty 1976

APPENDIX - LeDOUX VIE

This book hits the highlights of my life and gave some hint of other activities. For example the "Hi Bye" greeting by my 3 year old son when I returned from one of my trips made me think I was neglecting my family As the first Navy Civil Engineer to be involved in the nuclear business, traveling was necessary. My Australia trip was covered to some extent in the book but other trips to Austria and England and contact with many others in France, Germany, Japan and even Israel were not discussed in detail, if at all. As Director of the Navy Shore Based Nuclear Power Program I gained an international reputation. This  is not some form of boasting, just the way things worked out. The purpose of this appendix is to show a sampling of the letters and documents that touch on this activity. Some of these documents go back before I even entered the Navy. The letter from Judge Bruner is an example. Some are quite old and may not reproduce well. Above is the **Renault mentioned in the story.**

1. Alameda County DA letter for plane spotting work. May 28, 1942
2. Judge Brunner letter of recommendation April 22. 1943
3. Governor Warren letter June 12,1947
4. Admiral Meade letter of 11 April 1957
5. Society of American Military Engineers, Toulmin Medal 1960
6. De Leuw, Cather & Company letter October 25, 1961
7. University of New Mexico letter December 21,1961
8. Assistant Secretary of Navy commendation for CECOS April 27, 1962
9. Commonwealth of Australia letter 5ᵗʰ April 1965
10. White House letter 5 May 1965
11. Commendation for Achievement 1966
12. Director of Civil Defense letter recommending Dexter Award Nov1, 1966
13. Atomic Energy Research Establishment (England) letter 8ᵗʰ December 1966
14. Meritorious Unit Commendation for Navy Nuclear Power Unit
15. Admiral Corradi letter on CDR promotion 19 October 1962
16. Byrd Station Society Certificate 6 Nov 1964
17. Admiral Husband letter on retirement 23 June 1967
18. **Virginia Tech Emeritus award**

HONORS AND AFFILIATIONS

Member, National Academy of Science Committee
Member, White House Engineering Advisory Board
Secretary of Navy Award for Engineering
Navy Commendation for Work at Research Laboratory
Sesseion Chairman, Nuclear Symposium, Harwell, England
Session Chairman, Radioisotope Generator Symposium, Vienna, Austria
Navy Meritorius Unit Citation for McMurdo Operations
Associate Professor, Emeritus, Virginia Tech
Excellence in Teaching Award, Virginia Tech
President, Rosslyn Business Association

RALPH E. HOYT
DISTRICT ATTORNEY

OFFICE OF
DISTRICT ATTORNEY
OF
ALAMEDA COUNTY
OAKLAND, CALIFORNIA

J. FRANK COAKLE
CHIEF ASSISTANT

IN YOUR REPLY KINDLY
REFER TO FILE NO. _____

May 28th, 1942.

Mr. Jack C. LeDoux,
225 W. Broadmoor,
San Leandro, Calif.

Dear Mr. LeDoux:

I am enclosing herewith your Identification Card
as a member of the Ground Observation Corps of the Aircraft
Warning Service. I would suggest that you carry this card
with you at all times.

Brigadier General Kepner who has succeeded General
William Ord Ryan as Commanding Officer of the Fourth
Interceptor Command flew from March Field to Oakland last
April 6 and inspected several of the Observation Posts in
this area together with Major Gray. General Kepner compli-
mented the work of the Ground Observation Corps in Alameda
County and stressed the importance of this highly necessary
branch of the service.

I wish to extend to you my sincere personal thanks
for the time and effort you have devoted to a service so
vital to the safety of our country.

Very truly yours,

Ralph E. Hoyt

County Director
Aircraft Warning Service.

REH:njp
Enc.
3232 R1

JUSTICE'S COURT
EDEN TOWNSHIP
MASONIC TEMPLE BUILDING
TELEPHONE TRINIDAD 0122
SAN LEANDRO, CALIFORNIA

A. W. BRUNER
JUSTICE OF THE PEACE

PAUL J. DEMPSEY
CLERK

April 22, 1943

Office of Naval Procurement
703 Market Street
San Francisco, California

Gentlemen:

Mr. John C. LeDoux of this city informs me that he is
applying for a V-12 training. It is with a great deal
of satisfaction that I recommend for your consideration
Mr. LeDoux's application.

Mr. LeDoux graduated from the San Leandro High School
in the June, 1942 class, and during the time he was in
high school made an enviable record as a leader and student. He was President of his class, President of the
student body, and on several occasions Secretary of the
same. He is honest, sincere, intelligent, and has a
splendid reputation in this community. His loyalty to
this country cannot be questioned.

His father has been a police officer in San Leandro during the 12 years I have served as judge, and I have,
therefore, had a very good opportunity to know the family,
including the applicant. From my personal knowledge I am
of the opinion that if accepted by you Mr. LeDoux will be
of great service to his country and a credit to this city.

Respectfully yours,

AWB:LF

EARL WARREN
GOVERNOR

State of California
GOVERNOR'S OFFICE
SACRAMENTO

June 12, 1947

Mr. John C. LeDoux
285 West Broadmoor
San Leandro, California

My dear Ensign:

I was happy to receive the
announcement of your graduation from
Annapolis and congratulate you on having
realized your ambition. I can appreciate
how proud of you are your father and all
your family.

With best wishes for success
in your chosen career, I am

Sincerely,

Governor

EW:pz

CHIEF OF CIVIL ENGINEERS
DEPARTMENT OF THE NAVY
WASHINGTON

11 April 1957

My dear Lieutenant Ledoux:

I am just reading the April issue of our CEC
BULLETIN, and want to tell you how much I enjoyed
your article on the Nuclear Engineering Course at
Oak Ridge.

It was a fine thought that you, as the first
CEC selectee for this program, should write up your
experiences and reactions, and I read your article
with great interest.

Of course, I particularly enjoyed your considered
appraisal that life in the Civil Engineer Corps
compares most favorably with what the majority of
civilian engineers seem to enjoy.

My compliments on your excellent article, and
very best wishes for your continued success and
happiness.

Sincerely yours,

R. H. Meade
Rear Admiral, CEC, USN

Liuetenant J. C. Ledoux, CEC, USN
c/o ORSORT X-10
Oak Ridge, Tennessee

The MILITARY ENGINEER

AND The Society of American Military Engineers

RELEASE NO. 6111
April 26, 1961

808 Mills Building, Washington 6, D. C

Telephone: EXecutive 3-3370

●

NATIONAL AWARD FOR MILITARY ENGINEERING WRITING, 1960

The Society of American Military Engineers announces the award of the

Toulmin Medal

to

LT. COMDR. J. C. LeDOUX

for

his article "Nuclear Power: Promise and Problems"

judged the best article published in

THE MILITARY ENGINEER for 1960

The Toulmin Medal, named for Col. H. A. Toulmin who, through his interest in encouraging engineers to write, founded the award in 1932, is offered annually to the author of the article selected by a committee of judges as the best published in THE MILITARY ENGINEER during the calendar year.

Presentation will be made at the Annual Military Engineer Dinner of The Society on May 15, 1961, at the Mayflower Hotel.

Biog. Notes:

John C. LeDoux, Lieutenant Commander, Civil Engineer Corps, U. S. Navy, is the Executive Officer of the U. S. Naval School, CEC Officers, Port Hueneme, California. Prior to this duty he was the director of the Nuclear Division of the Naval Civil Engineering Laboratory there. He was born in Portland, Oregon, in 1924. He is a graduate of the U. S. Naval Academy with a B.S. degree, holds a B.C.E. degree from Rensselaer Polytechnic Institute, and a M.S. degree from the Navy Post Graduate School at Monterey. He was also a student at the Oak Ridge School of Reactor Technology for nuclear reactor engineering. During his career in the Navy he has had construction and maintenance assignments on both the east and west coasts and sea duty in the Pacific.

HONORABLE MENTION FOR THE TOULMIN MEDAL

Honorable mention is given to the following:

J. W. O'Meara for "Saline Water Conversion," March-April 1960

Brig. Gen. A. K. Sibley and William H. McNeice for "Harnessing the Tides," January-February 1960

Comdr. W. J. Christensen for "Nuclear Power for Navy Shore Bases," May-June 1960

DE LEUW, CATHER & COMPANY
ENGINEERS
WESTERN OFFICE
1256 MARKET STREET
SAN FRANCISCO 2, CALIFORNIA
UNDERHILL 1-1302

October 25, 1961

Lt. Commander J. C. LeDoux
Civil Engineer Corps
U.S. Naval Construction Battalion Center
Port Hueneme, California

Dear Commander Le Doux:

We have just finished the work in Class No. 2, "Building Analysis for Fallout Protection," and are writing this letter to express to you our sincere appreciation for the instruction received both from yourself and the members of your staff.

We found it a stimulating experience to be privileged to work with, even for such a short period, so dedicated and knowledgeable a group of men.

Again, please accept our commendation for the high quality of the work that is being done and our gratitude for the opportunity to have attended.

Yours very truly,

B. A. Lewis
F. L. ReQua
Staff Engineers

LR:fl

PLANT DEPARTMENT
THE DIRECTOR

December 21, 1961

LCDR John C. LEDOUX, CEC, USN
Executive Officer
US Naval Civil Engineering Officer's School
Port Hueneme, California

Dear Commander LEDOUX:

I guess you thought I'd forgotten to write you
personally, but I've been waiting to send you a
little reminder of your visit to New Mexico.
I hope you like the bow tie being forwarded under
separate cover. This tie is made by Zuni Craftsmen
and will give you a distinctly Southwestern motif
when you're in your mufti.

Commander, again I want to express the sincere
appreciation of our entire Superintendent-Foreman
group for your outstanding presentation. Your
contribution to our panel discussion was also
a distinct asset and a very helpful addition to
this varied group.

I hope you will keep in mind we do want a copy of
your presentation, as I have received a number of
requests for it.

With my best personal regards for the holiday season,
I remain,

Yours very truly,

M. F. Enfield
Director

MFF/jb

ASSISTANT SECRETARY OF DEFENSE
WASHINGTON 25, D.C.

APR 2 7 1962

MEMORANDUM FOR THE SECRETARY OF THE NAVY

SUBJECT: Civil Defense Courses Conducted by U. S. Navy
           Civil Engineer Corps Officers School

    During the period from September 18, 1961 through February 16,
1962, the U. S. Navy Civil Engineer Corps Officers School, Port Hueneme,
California, conducted a series of intensive two-week courses in fallout
shelter analysis for professional architects and engineers. These
courses were initiated at the request of the Office of Civil Defense,
Department of Defense, and have provided effective support for the
national shelter program. Similar courses have been conducted by only
eight universities and two military officers schools throughout the
country.

    The success of the national fallout shelter survey and subsequent
phases of the national shelter program will depend largely upon the
services of architects and engineers who have attended these courses.

    On behalf of the Secretary of Defense, I therefore, wish to commend
the U. S. Navy Civil Engineer Corps Officers School for conducting this
important professional level instruction which directly supports the
national civil defense effort.

Steuart L. Pittman

COMMONWEALTH OF AUSTRALIA

DEPARTMENT OF THE INTERIOR,

DIRECTORATE OF CIVIL DEFENCE

South Building,
Civic Offices,
CANBERRA.   A.C.T.

5th April, 1965.

AIR MAIL.

Dear Jack,

I was pleased to receive your letter
of March 3, 1965. It is very generous of your Navy not
to ask us to pay for fares for journeys which were under-
taken on our behalf. It reminds me of the many kindnesses
I received when I was operating with your 7th Fleet. We
should like to find another excuse for having you visit
us.

With kind regards,

Yours sincerely,

(A.E. Buchanan)
D i r e c t o r.

Commander J.C. LeDoux, CEC, USN,
Director, Nuclear Power Division,
Department of the Navy,
Bureau of Yards and Docks,
WASHINGTON, D.C. 20390   U.S.A.

THE WHITE HOUSE
WASHINGTON

5 May 1965

Dear Captain Christensen:

As Chairman of the Engineering Advisory Board, you were
authorized to convene the Board for the purpose of making
recommendations concerning planning and construction for
this office.

The Board met from the 28th to 31st of March inclusive.
The written report was received from the Board on the
22nd of April. It is apparent from a study of the report that
much work was done in a very short time. The report contains
a number of interesting observations and technical recommendations which I am sure will prove to be helpful.

It is requested, that as Chairman of the Board, you express
my appreciation to the members for their valuable contributions
to the planning for this office.

Sincerely yours,

JOHN V. JOSEPHSON
Naval Assistant to
the Military Aide

Captain W. J. Christensen, CEC, USN
Commanding Officer and Director
U. S. Naval Civil Engineering Laboratory
Port Hueneme, California - 93041

THE SECRETARY OF THE NAVY
WASHINGTON

COMMENDATION FOR ACHIEVEMENT

The Secretary of the Navy takes pleasure in commending

COMMANDER JOHN C. LE DOUX
GIVIL ENGINEER CORPS
UNITED STATES NAVY

for outstanding achievement in the superior performance of his duties in the field of nuclear engineering as set forth in the following

CITATION

During the period January 1962 to February 1963 while serving as Executive Officer, Civil Engineer Corps Officers School, and as Supervisory Nuclear Engineer, Office of Civil Defense, Commander (then Lieutenant Commander) LeDoux developed a simplified method of fallout radiation shielding analysis and design. This method provides architects and engineers with a graphic method of evaluating the interplay of the various shielding parameters, a quick means of analyzing complex structures, and a means of designing economic shields. The development of this design method was not required by the primary duties of Commander LeDoux and is the result of many off-duty hours of effort. His professional competence and untiring devotion to duty were in keeping with the highest traditions of the United States Naval Service.

Fred Garth

Secretary of the Navy

DEPARTMENT OF THE ARMY
OFFICE OF THE SECRETARY OF THE ARMY
OFFICE OF CIVIL DEFENSE
WASHINGTON, D.C. 20310

NOV 1 1966

Rear Admiral A. C. Husband, USN
Commander, Naval Facilities Engineering
    Command
Washington, D. C.

Dear Admiral Husband:

As you know, both the Office of Civil Defense and the Department of the
Navy are indebted to Cdr. John C. LeDoux for his pioneering work in
translating the state-of-the-art in radiation shielding into a rapid
means for engineering application. During the time that Cdr. LeDoux
was detailed to this office, it was felt that his contribution not only
to the Department of the Navy, but also to the entire civilian scientific engineering community of the Nation, was never fully acknowledged.

He was responsible for the development of the two enclosed technical
publications which have been used as the basis for teaching, qualifying,
and certifying over 11,500 fallout shelter analysts in the professions
of architecture or engineering. All of the analysts listed in the enclosed directory are, therefore, indebted to Cdr. LeDoux for his outstanding technical and scientific contribution toward their professional
development.

It appears that the Captain Robert Dexter Conrad award for scientific
achievement is most appropriate for adequate recognition of Cdr. LeDoux's
contribution. I would like to suggest his nomination for this award and
will provide any additional documentary data necessary to insure adequate
consideration is given for this well deserved recognition.

          Sincerely,

          William P. Durkee
          Director of Civil Defense

UKAEA

Your reference:

Our reference: AI/221/03

8th December 1966

Commander J.C. Ledoux,
Naval Facilities Engineering Command,
Washington D.C. 22030,
U.S.A.

Dear Commander Ledoux,

   I attach a copy of the transcript made from the tapes of the discussion at the Symposium. If you have no serious objection to what is attributed to you, this will be printed in the Symposium proceedings as it stands. If you do have any serious objections, would you please communicate with Dr. W.F. Haussermann, E.N.E.A., 38 Boulevard Suchet, Paris 16, France.

   I should like to take the opportunity of thanking you very much for your participation in the Symposium and especially for undertaking the Chairmanship of a Session at rather short notice.

   I look forward to meeting you again when you are next in this country.

Yours sincerely,

J. F. Pollock
Industrial Collaboration Office

dcf

CHIEF OF NAVAL OPERATIONS

      The Secretary of the Navy takes pleasure in presenting the
MERITORIOUS UNIT COMMENDATION to

NAVAL NUCLEAR POWER UNIT
FORT BELVOIR, VIRGINIA

for service as set forth in the following

CITATION:

      For meritorious service from 1 May 1964 to 1 March 1967 in the operation, modification, and support of the Nuclear Power Plant (PM-3A) at McMurdo Station, Antarctica. The PM-3A is the Navy's prototype shore-based nuclear power plant, and is the only plant of this nature which operates in such an isolated environment and replaces each crew each year. During this period, the Navy Nuclear Power Unit effected extensive plant modifications, plant redesign work, and changes in operating procedures, to achieve the operational reliability and availability required. These efforts involved such complex nuclear-engineering applications as whole-core refueling, control-rod driven mechanism modification, nuclear instrumentation improvements, identification and solution of the tritium problem, radioactive waste disposal system modification, and broken control-rod replacement. Due to these plant improvements and the high degree of technical competence and training of the PM-3A crews, the plant established a military record of 141 days of continous power operations, and completed the first United States land water desalting system operating with a nuclear plant. The initiative, professional competence, and devotion to duty displayed by the officers and men of the Naval Nuclear Power Unit were in keeping with the highest traditions of the United States Naval Service.

All personnel attached to and serving with Naval Nuclear Power Unit, Fort Belvoir, Virginia, during the period designated above, or any part thereof, and who were actually present and participating in the operations as outlined, are hereby authorized to wear the Meritorious Unit Commendation Ribbon.

For the Secretary,

T. H. Moorer

T. H. Moorer
Admiral, United States Navy
Chief of Naval Operations

CHIEF OF CIVIL ENGINEERS
DEPARTMENT OF THE NAVY
WASHINGTON

19 October 1962

Dear Jack:

I was delighted indeed to see your name on the list of officers selected for promotion to the grade of Commander in the Civil Engineer Corps. It is gratifying to know that the excellence of your performance has been recognized by the Board and has contributed to your selection.

Along with my congratulations, I would remind you of the greater responsibilities which your new rank will bring. It will require your further development in leadership as a Navy officer, and improvement in your professional abilities as an engineer.

I wish you continued success on your upward path.

Sincerely,

P. Corradi
Rear Admiral, CEC, USN

LCDR John C. LeDoux, CEC, USN
c/o Chief of Military Personnel
  Section
Personnel Branch
Office of the Secretary of Defense
Washington 25, D. C.

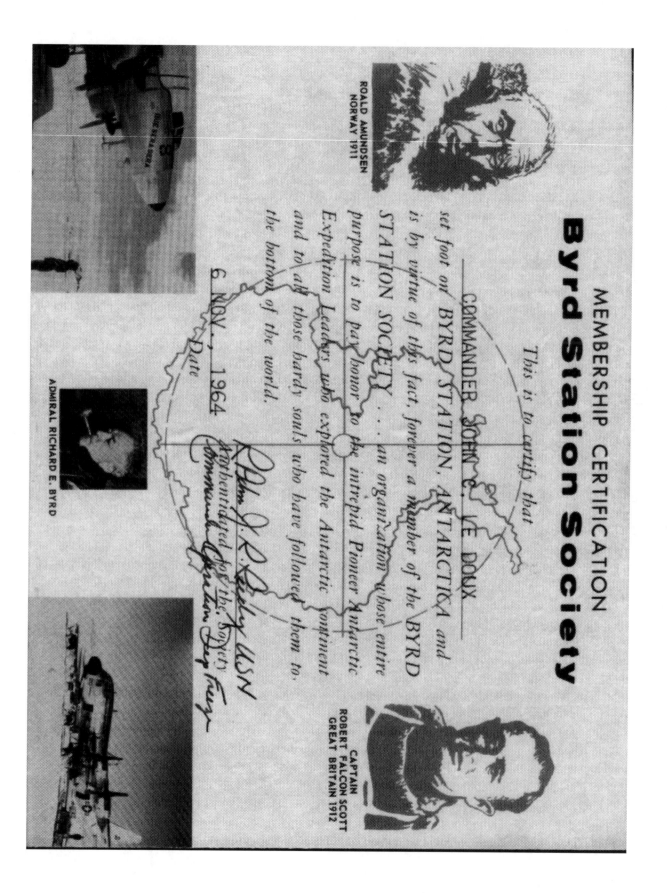

MEMBERSHIP CERTIFICATION

Byrd Station Society

This is to certify that

COMMANDER JOHN C. LE DOUX

set foot on BYRD STATION, ANTARCTICA and
is by virtue of this fact, forever a member of the BYRD
STATION SOCIETY . . . an organization whose entire
purpose is to pay honor to the intrepid Pioneer Antarctic
Expedition Leaders who explored the Antarctic continent
and to all those hardy souls who have followed them to
the bottom of the world.

6 NOV., 1964
Date

Robert J. R. Berry USN
Authenticated for the Byrd
Commander Byrd Station Society

ROALD AMUNDSEN
NORWAY 1911

ADMIRAL RICHARD E. BYRD

ROBERT FALCON SCOTT
CAPTAIN
GREAT BRITAIN 1912

23 June 1967

Dear Jack:

As you transfer to the retired list of the Navy, I want
to express the appreciation of a grateful Corps for your
many personal and professional contributions.

You have served in many demanding positions throughout
your career. In every assignment, and in particular those
assignments associated with our Nuclear Engineering Program,
you have performed in an outstanding manner that has reflected
great credit on your abilities as a professional engineer
and manager.

As you begin another career, I join with your fellow officers
in wishing you the best of everything in your future endeavors.
It is our hope that the friendships fostered over the years
will prove lasting and that our comardeship will continue
through the years to come.

Sincerely,

A. C. Husband
Rear Admiral, CEC, USN

Commander J. C. LeDoux, CEC, USN
Naval Facilities Engineering Command,
 Headquarters
Department of the Navy
Washington, D. C. 20390

Virginia Polytechnic Institute and State University

The Visitors of the Virginia Polytechnic Institute and State University in profound appreciation for 11 years of significant leadership and outstanding service in behalf of the University salute

John Carter DeVour, Associate Professor Emeritus

who as

Associate Professor of Engineering Fundamentals

has been dedicated to duty, generous in the investment of time and talents, and loyal to the cause of higher education.

Date: June 1, 1992

Margie W. Thomas
Clerk

_____
Rector